Marxist Economics for Socialists
A Critique of Reformism

*Politics is the concentrated
expression of economics*

LENIN

John Harrison

Marxist Economics
for Socialists
A Critique of Reformism

Pluto  Press

First published 1978 by Pluto Press Limited
Unit 10 Spencer Court, 7 Chalcot Road, London NW1 8LH

Copyright © Pluto Press 1978

ISBN 0 86104 015 5 paperback
    0 86104 016 3 hardback

Photoset by Red Lion Setters, Holborn, London

Printed in England by Billing & Sons Limited,
Guildford and Worcester

Cover designed by Oscar Zarete

Contents

**Part Two. Capitalism and the Productive Forces:
the Critique of Social Democracy**

Preface

This book is about capitalism and reformism: the way of organising production which dominates the world today and the approach to changing it which dominates the labour movement. It is highly critical of both. It is also an introduction to marxist economics written for socialists. The relationship between these topics is one theme of the book.

Many people helped to write it. Di Parkin wrote almost an entire first draft from tapes of educationals given in the Greyhound pub in Oxford in the spring of 1975. The book was originally to be a joint effort and she contributed much. The final result is dedicated to her. Nora Hickey and Glen Park also drafted sections. Philip Armstrong, Andrew Glyn, Marcus Giaquinto, Anne Philips, Tim Putnam, Julia Stallibras and David Whitfield made valuable comments. Richard Kuper, as editor, gave much useful advice while gently cajoling me into finishing it. Eva Kaluzynska helped improve the style enormously, eliminating some grotesque metaphors and untangling eccentric grammar and spelling. My thanks to them all.

Oxford
July 1977

Introduction

1. Politics, Economics and History

1. Marx and the Socialists

Marx's central concerns were political. While that is hardly news to anyone, it does raise the question of why he chose to spend the best years of his life, as he put it, writing about the economic workings of capitalism. For much of this time he did not belong to a political organisation. When politically active, he complained that this interfered with his work on his economics.

The answer is that his economics had a political purpose. It was of immediate relevance to the labour movement in the second half of the nineteenth century.

Marx developed his economics as a criticism of ideas held by politically advanced workers. In his view, the working class failed to come to power during the revolutionary upsurge that swept across Europe in 1848 primarily because it was small in relation to other social groups. This prevented it from developing a clear political perspective of its own. The ideas of those who emerged in the leadership of the workers' movement after 1848 were, in his opinion, confused. If left unchallenged, they would continue to mislead the class politically when it grew in numbers.

Convinced that these ideas were taking root, Marx began to produce a systematic critique of them. He concentrated on the work of Proudhon and his followers, whom he called *bourgeois socialists* (or often just socialists) because their views were the most influential.[1] One result of this work was *Capital*.

Proudhonism, or bourgeois socialism, was not the only pre-marxist school of socialist thought. Marx distinguishes two other main categories.

The *feudal socialists* were representatives of tne aristocracy, the old ruling class displaced by the emergence of capitalism. Marx describes their oppositlon to the system as follows:

> In order to arouse sympathy ... (they) were obliged to lose sight, apparently, of their own interests, and to formulate their indict-ment against the bourgeoisie in the interest of the exploited working class alone. Thus the aristocracy took their revenge by singing lampoons on their new master, and whispering in his ears sinister prophecies of coming catastrophe.[2]

The *utopian socialists*, on the other hand, were those who:

> wish to attain their end by peaceful means, and endeavour,' by small experiments, necessarily doomed to failure, and by the force of example, to pave the way for the new social Gospel ... They still dream of ... founding ... 'Home Colonies', of setting up duo-decimo editions of the New Jerusalem - and to realise all these castles in the air they are compelled to appeal to the feelings and purses of the bourgeoisie.[3]

To Marx, neither group seemed a serious obstacle to the political development of the working class. Feudal socialism romanticised a past historical period. It was attractive only to members of the old ruling class still haunting the present. Marx was scathing about these people's influence within the labour movement:

> In pointing out that their mode of exploitation was different to that of the bourgeoisie, the feudalists forget that they exploited under circumstances and conditions that were quite different, and that are now antiquated ... But the people, so often as it joined them, saw on their hindquarters the old feudal coat of arms, and deserted with loud and irreverent laughter.[4]

Utopian socialism was no more dangerous. Although it did not attempt to turn the clock back in the ludicrous manner of the feudalists, it was equally unable to offer a realistic way forward. By the time Marx was writing, utopianism had degenerated to little more than a conviction that it would be nicer if people had a nicer world to live in and were nicer to each other. Its advocates had always devised blue-prints for a perfect world and attempted to bring it about by setting up model communities which would, they hoped, by their example, persuade others to join. But the more elaborate the plans for a perfect world became, the less able were the planners to relate realistically to the world as it was. The utopians came to view the growing class struggle between proletariat and bourgeoisie (workers and capitalists) as at best a distraction from the task of building socialism in one village and at worst an obstacle to it:

> In proportion as the modern class struggle develops ... this fantastic standing apart from the contest ... lose(s) all practical value and all theoretical justification. Therefore, although the originators of these systems were, in many respects, revolutionary, their disciples have, in every case, formed mere reactionary sects ... They, therefore, violently oppose all political action on the part of the working class; such action, according to them, can only result from blind unbelief in the new Gospel.[5]

In contrast, bourgeois socialism did not merely counterpose an alternative ideal society - based on a revival of feudalism or the creation of workers' co-operatives - to the existing one. Its ideas and practice related, albeit in a confused way, to the real world. Its supporters played an active role in the class struggle. Thus proudhonist ideas seemed to many workers to make sense.

Marx did not doubt the bourgeois socialists' subjective commitment. He had great personal respect for Proudhon, who underwent considerable hardship to study and carry out political activity. Neither Proudhon nor his followers were deliberately misleading the proletariat. But, because they failed to understand the real nature of capitalist society, they were incapable of devising a viable strategy for transforming it.

Marx devoted a good deal of time to demonstrating that certain bourgeois-socialist proposals were misconceived and impractical. For example, he developed much of his analysis of the workings of capitalism in lengthy critiques of a plan to abolish money, which the proudhonists believed responsible for many social evils. But these specific criticisms were based on a more fundamental disagreement.

The bourgeois socialists believed it possible to modify the existing system, so as to produce a free and equal society.

Socialism, to them, meant precisely this. Marx did not believe it possible. He devoted most of the latter part of his life to producing a scientific analysis of capitalism that would both support his arguments against bourgeois socialism and establish the real requirements for achieving freedom and equality.

In Marx's view, the proudhonists' central political mistake flowed from a weakness in their method of analysis. They failed to examine capitalism in a historical context. Because they did not see capitalism as a specific stage in the development of human society, they could not distinguish clearly between features peculiar to it and those also found in other societies.

The failure to place capitalism historically led the bourgeois socialists into two major errors of analysis. The first was a confusion between capitalism and another logically possible system of production for sale - or *commodity* production - which Marx called *simple commodity production*. In such a system, everyone would work on their own account, producing and selling goods. While this is a perfectly conceivable way of organising economic activity, it is not one which has ever existed historically. The development of independent craftsmen producing goods for sale did play a part in the breakup of feudalism. But the spreading of buying and selling through society gave rise to capitalism rather than to simple commodity production. By the time Marx was writing, such self-employed craftsmen - or *artisans* - were being rapidly displaced by the growth of capital.

As well as failing to understand the changes undergone by commodity production in the course of its development from an embryonic artisanal stage to a fully-fledged capitalist one, the proudhonists also did not recognise that the *whole period* of production for sale was only a stage in human history; that it had been preceded by different economic systems and could, in turn, be followed by others not based on commodity production.

Thus the bourgeois socialists treated institutions and activities peculiar to certain societies as eternal. Activities such as buying and selling, for example - specific to societies based on commodity production - were in their view as inevitable and immutable as the existence of gravitational pull.

The proudhonists' politics followed logically from their un-historical analysis. Confusion between capitalism and simple commodity production, which unlike capitalism need not involve unequal or coercive relationships between people, led them to believe it possible to modify capitalism so as to achieve a free and equal society. Confusion between features specific to commodity production and those common to all social systems restricted them to a programme for reforming a society based on production for sale: they simply could not see that any other economic system was possible.

By arguing that capitalism need not be exploitative, the proudhonists were in effect defending the system. Their attitude to capitalism as a way of organising production was at root complementary to that of the bourgeoisie. Most defenders of the system would admit that it produces frictions and suffers from the excesses of unscrupulous individuals. Many would welcome schemes to reduce these so as to improve overall efficiency. Marx puts the point well:

> The bourgeoisie naturally conceives the world in which it is supreme to be the best; and bourgeois socialism develops this comfortable conception into various more or less complete systems. In requiring the proletariat to carry out such a system, and thereby to march straightway into the social New Jerusalem, it but requires in reality, that the proletariat should remain within the bounds of existing society, but should cast away all its hateful ideas concerning the bourgeoisie.[6]

This would be of purely historical interest if the approach to politics underlying bourgeois socialism had disappeared, as feudalism and utopianism have.[7] But it has not. Few workers today would defend the classic proudhonist view that one or two central reforms could transform capitalism into a free and equal society. But the majority would argue a weaker but similar line: that it is possible to achieve substantial and permanent gains for the working class within capitalism and thereby move gradually towards such a society.

This general approach is known as *reformism*. Its most influential contemporary variant is *social democracy*.

2. Historical Materialism

The bourgeois socialists' political weaknesses arose from their inability to see capitalism historically. In contrast, Marx's economic analysis locates capitalist society as a stage in human history. His theory of historical development and his economics are therefore interdependent. Neither can be understood fully in isolation from the other.

Marx's theory of history is usually known as historical materialism. It is *historical* in that a society can only be understood in the context of its history; by recognising it to be a stage in a process of social development which has passed through previous phases and will continue through subsequent ones. It is *materialist* because the theory takes as its point of departure the material pre-conditions for human survival: the interaction between human beings and nature which satisfies human needs. [8]

Both human activity and favourable natural conditions are essential to this interaction. But Marx places the emphasis on the expenditure of human effort because the using up of mental and physical energy is the real cost to humanity of transforming nature to produce useful objects. He calls this process of transformation *production*.

From the earliest periods of history - when human life was barely distinguishable from that of animals and production consisted of simple hunting and gathering - to the present, the development of production is the most significant factor in human history.

Marx considered human beings' capacity to transform nature to be the chief basis upon which to distinguish them from animals. Language and conceptual thought - the human attributes on which bourgeois social science places the most emphasis - are a consequence of productive activity, as are changes in social arrangements. The best single indicator of human progress is therefore progress in production. Marx calls the extent to which a society has developed its capacity to transform nature the *level of development of the productive forces*.

The development of the productive forces has been a complex and continuous process. But it has been marked by two really significant changes. The first, usually known as the *neolithic revolution*, was the development of agriculture: groups of people, who for many thousands of years had lived from hand to mouth by hunting and gathering, began to intervene in the processes of nature to satisfy needs over a longer time span. They began to plan seeds, to tend crops and to raise animals to ensure a constant food supply.

The second major development, usually known as the *industrial revolution*, saw the development of production by the systematic use of machinery.

The development of production has been accompanied by changes in the way it is organised; that is, by developments in the inter-connections between people engaged in transforming nature. Thus relations between people who own land and raise crops for their own consumption, for example, are substantially different from those which exist under capitalism, where most people work for capitalists who pay them wages which they then exchange for goods produced by people working for other capitalists. Marx calls interconnections between people *social relations*.

Marx uses this *materialist methodology* - the way of looking at historical development which begins from the interaction between human beings and nature essential to human survival - to develop the actual *theory* of historical materialism. This consists of two main propositions.

The first is that the way in which production is organised determines the general character of all other social institutions and processes. This is a static principle. It applied to relationships within a given society, not to the process of historical change. According to this principle, sound analyses of the legal and political systems or of the ways of looking at the world that characterise a particular society must take as their starting point an examination of the economic system, because that is the chief determinant of other aspects of society.

Marx once illustrated this principle with the metaphor of *base* and *superstructure*: the economic base of a society largely determines the nature of non-economic institutions and processes, which constitute the superstructure. The relationship between the foundation of a building and the structure built upon it provides a helpful image. But it is important to remember that it was intended as no more than that. If interpreted too literally, it implies - and has led many marxists to infer - that all changes in the superstructure can be deduced from, or reduced to, changes in the economic base, the prevailing *mode of production*. This kind of *reductionism* diminishes the significance of superstructural elements and denies their capacity to act back upon the economic base.

Marx never argued that a straightforward one-to-one relationship exists between changes in economic processes and, say, legal and political systems. In fact he fought vigorously against such over-simplified interpretations of his theory - not to protect his academic reputation, but because he was aware of how politically dangerous they could be.

The other basic proposition of historical materialism is a dynamic rather than a static one. It is concerned with the process of change. According to this principle, major social changes occur because relations of production become at some point a hindrance to further development of the productive forces. After some time, a way of organising production ceases to be an effective way of increasing human beings' control over nature and must then give way to another economic system capable of encouraging further development. When this happens, there is a period of major social change which Marx calls a *social revolution*.

This conception differs from the everyday use of the term revolution. It is a major social change rather than a violent seizure of power. It may or may not *involve* such a seizure - Marx argued that the change from capitalism to socialism would - but it is not *defined* by it. Thus a military coup by a new section of the army in a country already under military rule does not constitute a social revolution. On the other hand, the historical process which transformed Western Europe from a feudal to a capitalist society, replacing the rule of the feudal aristocracy by that of the bourgeoisie - a process which in many countries took centuries and whose violence, though considerable, was often less apparent than that of the average military coup - was a social revolution. It brought about a far-reaching transformation of relationships within society.

It obviously follows from the first, static proposition of historical materialism that major social changes involve changes in the mode of production. The second proposition adds an explanation as to why such changes occur. An implication of it is that every mode of production goes through two phases: an early one when the relations of production act as a stimulus to the development of the productive forces and a late one when these relations have become a hindrance to the further development of people's ability to transform nature.

Imagine a land reform which freed serfs and gave them small plots of land. The effect would probably be to increase production because people would now be working full-time for themselves on land they owned, rather than for a feudal lord half the time, and would therefore have a greater incentive to devise more efficient farming techniques. The new relations of production would stimulate development of the productive forces. If, later on, important inventions took place which were capable of increasing agricultural production if undertaken on a large scale, such as irrigation works, then the fact that production was organised on the basis of small plots would become a barrier to further development of the productive forces.

Since the most important aspect and index of human development is the level of development of the productive forces, the early phase in the life of a mode of production can be described as *historically progressive* and the later phase as *nonprogressive*.

Marx's ideas about historical change should not be interpreted in too mechanical a way. Historical change is not a remote spectacle which people are entitled only to observe. Changes take place through human activity. Marx once put it this way: people make their own history but in definite circumstances which are not of their choosing. The value of historical materialism is its ability to explain those circumstances and thereby to allow people to shape the historical process in a conscious and effective manner.

In his simplest schema, Marx distinguishes three *broad* stages of human history. In the first, production was largely agricultural. Rural life predominated. Human beings had yet to cut the 'umbilical cord' with nature. This stage included primitive agricultural communities, feudalism and slavery. Social relations were largely ones of personal dependence: slaves and serfs were bound to particular masters for life. Marx says of the serf that he appears 'as an aspect of property in land itself, as an appendage of the soil' and of the slave that 'the worker is nothing but a living labour machine'. This stage began with the first great development in the productive forces, the neolithic revolution. Marx sometimes calls this stage the period of *natural economy*.

The second stage is that in which goods are produced for sale. This initially took the form of artisanal production. Later, capitalism evolved. People no longer produce for the direct satisfaction of their own needs - consuming, say, food they have produced - but specialise in making a single product for sale. They satisfy most of their needs by buying from other people. This development of specialised trades is usually called an increase in *the division of labour*. This stage is the period of commodity production.

The move from the first stage to the second broke down the social relations of personal dependency which characterised natural economy. Workers under capitalism, for example, are free to change employers, whereas serfs and slaves remained the property of a single master throughout their lives. Since, in a system of commodity production, people depend for their survival on being able to buy and sell goods, *impersonal dependence on the market* replaces personal dependency in this second phase. Although workers are free to change employers under capitalism, they nevertheless depend for their living on some capitalist being willing to employ them.

The move from the first stage to the second also cut the umbilical cord with nature. Production became mainly nonagricultural and, instead of rural life predominating, the rapid growth of cities occurred. The consolidation of this stage in Europe came with the second great development in the productive forces, the industrial revolution.

The final stage Marx envisaged was that of socialism and communism. After a period of transition while this was established, the tyranny of the market would be replaced by the direct and collective control of production and of all other aspects of life by the producers. Coercive state institutions, like police forces and armies, would slowly disappear. People would eventually transform nature to satisfy their wants on the basis of 'from each according to his ability, to each according to his needs'.

3. Marx's Economics and Reformism: an Outline

The political purpose and theory of history underlying Marx's studies influenced his analysis of the capitalist mode of production. Political priorities made it imperative that he produce both a thorough-going critique of proudhonism and a realistic strategy for achieving socialism. Historical materialism suggested that these objectives could only be achieved by analysing capitalism as a stage in the historical process. The structure of this book has been shaped by similar considerations.

Part one is organised around the first proposition of historical materialism. It examines the principle features of commodity production and the ways in which they influence non-economic aspects of society. Its political focus is a critique of bourgeois socialism, the type of reformism predominant in Marx's time, and of the residue of these ideas which continues to influence the labour movement.

One object is to distinguish features specific to commodity production from those common to all modes of production - necessary aspects of transforming nature however the process is organised from those peculiar to the second great phase of human history. This is important politically because reformists tend to treat historically specific features of commodity production as natural and eternal facts of life.

A second purpose is to distinguish features specific to simple commodity production, those specific to capitalism and those common to both. This is important politically because of the proudhonists' confusion between these two logically possible types of commodity production.

A third task is to establish the nature of social relations within capitalism. This is crucial politically. If relationships between people in production are essentially free and equal, the proudhonist perspective is perfectly reasonable. Reforms to remove such inequalities as exist would improve the operation of the system and create a free and equal society. If, on the other hand, capitalist social relations are necessarily unequal or coercive, reforms are insufficient to create such a society and the bourgeois socialists were misleading both themselves and the working class by suggesting otherwise.

More mundanely, this part is also concerned with how capitalism works. It is important to know this, not in order to devise ways to make it work better - which is why bourgeois economists and some reformists examine its operation - but to assess critically specific proposals for reforms; to distinguish between schemes which, if implemented, would benefit workers and ones which would be against their interests.

Part one closes with an examination of ways in which commodity exchange affects the rest of society; how - to return to the metaphor - the economic base determines the superstructure. This fulfils two important political functions. One is to indicate the historically specific nature of many institutions and activities. This provides a justification for a more radical approach to many aspects of everyday life than that offered by reformists. Secondly, by showing how the mode of production influences people's ideas, it gives an insight into the pervasive influence of many incorrect notions. Marx was very concerned with this. He referred to some of his economic writings as a *critique of political economy*: an exposure of the mystified ways in which economists in particular think about capitalism.

Part two is structured around the second proposition of historical materialism. It examines the development of capitalism from progressive to non-progressive phases. Its political focus is a critique of social democracy, the type of reformism predominant today.

This part opens with an examination of the progressive role which early capitalism played. A discussion of the implications of this for political strategy follows. These two sections are important for understanding the origins of reformism and its transformation from a proudhonist to a social democratic form.

The remainder of the book is concerned with the development of capitalism and reformism during the twentieth century. The division of the workers' movement into social democratic (reformist) and revolutionary camps in the opening decades of this century is located in disagreements over the limits to capitalism's historically progressive role. The implications for political strategy of the different analyses are discussed.

The final chapter examines post-war developments. It relates both the changes of form and the increase in influence of social democracy to the relative stabilisation of capitalism. In conclusion, there is a discussion of the implications of the present crisis for the future of both capitalism and reformism.

An analysis of the history of capitalist development and its inherent limits is central to the building of a revolutionary alternative to reformism within the labour movement. It was just such an analysis - especially of the development of the producers themselves, the working class - which enabled Marx to progress beyond a moral critique of the way things were. As a revolutionary, his concern was to establish how they could be changed. Unlike the utopians, he was neither puzzled nor disappointed by the growth of the class struggle. He welcomed it. He recognised that capitalism, by developing the working class, was creating its own gravediggers.

Main characteristics of five possible modes of production

Mode of production	Class of producers	Exploiting class	Element of production owned by exploiting class	Purpose of production
Slavery	Slaves	Slave owners	Producers	Use value; occasional exchange value
Feudalism	Serfs	Landlords	Land	Use value
Simple commodity production	Artisans	None	None	Exchange value
Capitalism	Proletarians	Capitalists	Machines	Exchange value
Socialism	Workers	None	None	Use value

Do producers organise production?	Is there free and equal exchange?	Do producers receive all they produce?	Does it appear so from within capitalist ideology?	Economic causes leading to higher mode of production	Which mode of production follows?
No	Yes, for commodity owners	No	No. Looks as though they receive none	Generalisation of exchange	Commodity production
Yes, on own land, individually. No, on lord's land	Yes, for commodity owners	No	No. Looks as if they don't receive product of work on lord's land	Development of exchange	Commodity production
Yes, individually	Yes	Yes, individually	Yes	Extension of exchange to include labour power as commodity	Capitalism
No	Yes	No	Yes. Profits appear to reward contribution of capital	Socialisation of production. Crises	Socialism
Yes, collectively	No exchange	Yes, collectively	No. Some goes for social purposes rather than to individuals	Development of productive forces towards abolition of scarcity	Communism

Part One

The social relations of commodity production: the critique of bourgeois socialism

2. Simple Commodity Production

This chapter looks at a logically possible way of carrying out economic activity which Marx called simple commodity production. There are two reasons for beginning with this. The first is expositional. Simple commodity production, as the name suggests, is a simpler form of commodity production than capitalism. As such, it provides a convenient way of examining features common to both systems without immediately encountering all the complexities of capitalism. The second reason is political. A confusion between simple commodity production and capitalism underlay many of the bourgeois socialists' errors. An understanding of both systems clarifies these mistakes.

The final section of the chapter contains a brief discussion of the relation between the model of simple commodity production and those real economic systems from which it is derived. An understanding of the historical context in which proudhonism arose renders comprehensible its widespread appeal.

1. The Nature of Simple Commodity Production

Imagine an idealised country village. The thatched cottages around the green buzz with activity. There is a blacksmith at his forge and a weaver at his loom; a butcher, a baker and maybe even a candlestick maker. All the requirements for life are produced in the village and surrounding farms. The community is self-contained and self-sufficient.

But no single inhabitant is self-sufficient. Nobody lives by consuming only goods they themselves produce. Saturday is market day. Farmers come in with cattle and vegetables, the cobbler has a shoe stall and the weaver sells cloth. People live by selling most of their produce and buying from other villagers.

What are the characteristic features of this way of organising production?

One is that the individual producers, usually known as artisans, own all the requirements for undertaking production. For production to take place in any system, the following elements are necessary:

1. *Labourers* - workers themselves
2. *Objects of labour* - materials to work on (land, wood, iron, etc.)
3. *Means of labour* - tools to work with (axes, saws, lathes, etc.)

Without these, no transformation of nature would be possible.

When analysing a society, it is important to discover who owns the various elements of production. They may be owned by the labourers themselves, in either an individual or a collective manner, or by another group of people. Any group other than the producers which owns a requirement for production constitutes an exploiting class in a society divided into classes.

Under slavery, the producers themselves are the property of slave owners. Under feudalism, the land - the most important object of labour in an agricultural society - is owned by feudal landlords. Under capitalism, the machines and factories - means of labour - are owned by capitalists. Slave owners, feudal land-lords and capitalists are exploiting classes in their respective societies.

By owning an element of production, an exploiting class is able to appropriate some goods produced by the labourers. For this to be possible, the productive forces must have developed sufficiently to permit the production of a *surplus*; that is, products over and above those required to keep the workers alive and to replace materials used up and tools worn out in production.

The chief exploiting class in a society is usually also the ruling class. A precondition for a group establishing itself in a position of political authority over others is its emancipation from the need to work to produce its own consumption requirements.

Under simple commodity production, all requirements for

production are owned by individual artisans. They are free and hence 'own' themselves. They own the land they work on, the buildings they work in and the tools they work with. The farmer owns land and a plough. The blacksmith owns his forge, anvil and metal. There is neither an exploiting nor a ruling class under simple commodity production. It is not a class society.

A second important characteristic of simple commodity production is that a developed *division of labour* exists. People do different jobs. They work on different objects of labour with different means of labour to produce different goods. The blacksmith hammers metal on his anvil to produce horseshoes. The cobbler shapes leather into shoes. They each specialise in producing a narrow range of goods. No one produces everything that he or she consumes.

A developed division of labour is not found in all economic systems. Under feudalism, for example, many serfs produced almost the whole range of goods necessary for their subsistence. They worked on their own land for so many days a week, producing their own food, and on the lord's land for the remaining days. Many people gathered their own fuel, made their own clothing and so on.

The division of labour relates closely to a third feature of simple commodity production: it is production for *exchange*. People specialise in making a narrow range of goods which they exchange for other people's specialities. Eventually, everyone emerges with a variety of goods to consume, although they themselves have produced only one type of article.

In the village, exchange takes place as follows. From Monday to Friday people work at their trades. The cobbler makes shoes, the farmers grow food and so on. Saturday is market day. The artisans set up stalls to sell their products and then spend the proceeds on goods from other stalls. They leave with a wide range of provisions for the following week.

Although production is common to all societies, production for exchange is not. The labourers may consume everything they produce. In some peasant societies, people live off crops they grow without exchanging anything. Even where producers do not consume all of their produce, the surplus is not necessarily exchanged. A ruling class may appropriate it without any exchange taking place. Under feudalism, for example, the lords simply keep the surplus produced by serfs' work on their land.

To understand the relation between production in general and production for exchange, Marx introduced the distinction between *use value* and *exchange value*.

The term use value has two senses. *A* use value is something which satisfies a human want and *the* use value it has is the property of satisfying a particular want. Thus a tape-recorder *is* a use value and the use value *of* a tape-recorder is its ability to record sounds.

The concept involves no moral or aesthetic considerations, no distinction between so-called natural and artificial needs. Goods that we today might regard as useless, or worse than useless, such as vaginal deodorants or clothes for animals, nevertheless constitute use values so long as somebody wants them.

A use value need not be a physical object. Singing has a use value providing someone enjoys it even though, when it is over, nothing tangible remains. Anything which satisfies anybody's wants is a use value.

Not all use values are the products of human labour. Air has a use value. It fulfils a human need - people die if they do not inhale it frequently - but no labour of transformation is involved. Air does not have to be produced. Almost all products of human labour are use values though.[1]

But not all use values are *exchange values*. Some have no exchange value because no one will swap or pay anything for them. A painter may, for instance, produce pictures which have no exchange value because nobody else likes them. For something to be an exchange value it must have a use value for someone other than the producer.

For production for exchange to take place, a division of labour must exist. Where everyone produces the same things, there is nothing to be gained by swapping or buying and selling. People may give each other occasional gifts, of course, but there is no basis for *systematic* exchange.

Although the production of exchange values cannot take place in the absence of a division of labour, the reverse is not the case. A division of labour may exist without production being for exchange. If people specialise, they need to consume other people's products. But the distribution of goods can be organised in different ways. For instance, in the village, instead of a market day, there could be a weekly meeting at which everyone discussed and voted on how the goods produced during that week were to be distributed among the inhabitants. A division of labour would still exist and people would still consume a wider range of things than they themselves produced. But there would not be any exchange in the sense of individual buying, selling or swapping.

Production for exchange, or the production of exchange values, is thus specific to certain modes of production. While the production of use values is common to all forms of human society, the production of exchange values is specific to the second great phase of human development. During the first phase, under natural economy, people produced for their own consumption and, often, to provide a tribute for a ruling class. During the third phase, that of socialism and communism, there will still be a division of labour (though a much less rigid one than exists today) and people will consume the products of others' work. But use values will not be exchanged on a market. Their allocation will be decided upon collectively and democratically by the producers, as in the example of the village meeting.

Marx called the period of human history that lies between natural economy and communism that of *commodity production*. A commodity is a use value which has exchange value. It is a use value which is produced for exchange - made to be swapped or sold on a market. The phase of commodity production is thus the period of history in which production is undertaken for exchange.

The relationship between the categories of 'things in general', use values and commodities is summarised in Diagram 1 (on page 34).

As use values, commodities differ from each other qualitatively. A carrot has different physical attributes from a car - it satisfies different needs. As exchange values, commodities differ

Diagram 1 **From things to commodities**

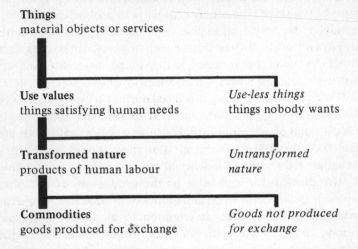

Things
material objects or services

Use values
things satisfying human needs

Use-less things
things nobody wants

Transformed nature
products of human labour

Untransformed nature

Commodities
goods produced for exchange

Goods not produced for exchange

from each other only quantitatively. They all fetch a price on the market. The only difference between them is that some fetch a higher price than others.

The seller of a commodity is interested only in its exchange value. He or she does not intend keeping the commodity and is concerned only about the price it will fetch. The buyer, on the other hand, is interested in both the use value of the object or service - as its qualities will determine how well it satisfies his or her wants - and in its exchange value; the more expensive it is, the less money will be left to buy other things.

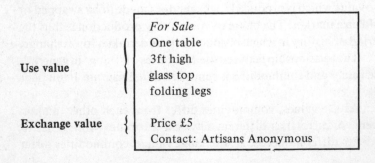

Use value

For Sale
One table
3ft high
glass top
folding legs

Exchange value

Price £5
Contact: Artisans Anonymous

These twin aspects of a commodity are clearly illustrated by simple advertisements, such as postcards in newsagents' windows.

To summarise, the main distinctive characteristics of simple commodity production are as follows. First, individual producers own all the requirements for undertaking production, and hence the system is not a class society. Second, a developed division of labour exists - people specialise in different jobs. Finally, production is undertaken for the exchange value of commodities - the price they will fetch on the market - rather than for their use values.

2. The Workings of the System

It is easy enough to understand how the system works for an individual artisan. Take the shoemaker, for example. He arrives on market day and sets up his stall. He sells his shoes for the highest price he can persuade people to pay and spends the money on leather, thread and so on to make more shoes and on food, clothing and other goods to keep himself alive and well so that he can work the following week. He shops around the market to buy these as cheaply as possible.

It is more difficult to discover how simple commodity production works as far as society as a whole is concerned. What ensures that various articles are produced in the proportions that the inhabitants require? There is no overall direction as to which goods are to be produced by whom. It seems perfectly possible that quite the wrong balance of goods might be produced. Suppose everyone decided to produce clothes one year, there would be no food. Or a village might find itself with ten blacksmiths and no cobbler.

A complex interrelationship exists between the production of different goods. If a certain number of shoes are to be produced not only are the right number of cobblers required but also sufficient farmers raising cattle and tanners turning the hides into leather. Tailors require cloth. Bakers need flour. If the desired balance of consumer goods is to be produced, the necessary objects of labour must be available in the correct proportions.

The problem is to explain how the sum of individuals' decisions, made without consultation with each other on the basis of expectations about which trades will yield the highest income for a week's work, makes any overall social sense. How does a system which is *anarchic*, as Marx put it, avoid continually breaking down?[2] What, in the absence of any central planning, is the mechanism which allocates total human labour between the production of different commodities in workable proportions?

Marx's solution to this problem is the famous *law of value*. The rest of this section is devoted to an explanation of the operation of this law under simple commodity production.

The Law of Value - I

Artisans are interested only in the exchange value, or market price, of goods they produce. The product's use value does not concern them directly because they are not going to keep it. Thus they will be prepared to switch jobs if by doing so they earn more for their week's work. If a tailor sells his week's worth of clothes and receives very little for them but sees the cobbler getting much more for his shoes, he will switch trades and become a cobbler.

This behaviour is itself a product of commodity production. Since, in a system based on exchange, survival depends on receiving enough money to buy the necessities of life, a producer *must* switch to making something else if people will not pay enough for his or her existing products. To argue, as some people do, that, because people act in this way to get by in commodity producing societies, such behaviour must be intrinsic to human beings, is like arguing that because I speak French so as to get by when in France, French must be my normal language. In fact, both forms of behaviour have to be learnt (see chapter 4).

How is the income an artisan receives for having spent a week making trousers or shoes determined? Part of the answer is supply and demand.

Suppose our tailor comes to market with four pairs of trousers, as he does every week, and sets up his stall. He charges

£20 a pair, his normal price. This particular week, however, there are more tailors than usual, all trying to sell trousers. But only the normal number of people intend to buy them. The tailors fear that not all of them will be able to sell their entire output. Each then lowers the price of his trousers in an attempt to persuade people to buy from him, rather than from his competitors. As the price of trousers falls, people who had not planned to buy any that week change their mind, as they see how unusually cheap they are. As the price falls, demand increases. Either some trousers remain unsold or, if they are all sold, the price is lower than usual, say £10 a pair. Our tailor leaves with only £40 for his week's work, instead of his usual £80.

Perhaps the cobbler fared better. Say he came with four pairs of shoes and offered them for sale at £20 a pair. He realised that there were fewer shoes than usual for sale; more people wanted to buy shoes at £20 a pair than were available. He raised the price. As the price went up, people who had intended to buy shoes changed their mind. Eventually, he found he could not raise the price further and still sell all his shoes. Perhaps the price rose to £30 a pair. He left with £120 for a week's work instead of his usual £80.

The unfortunate tailor, seeing the cobbler selling all of his shoes at a high price, would switch to the production of shoes. Within a short while, the supply of trousers would be reduced and that of shoes increased. This would have the effect of pushing the price of shoes down and that of trousers up.

In this way, the system tends towards a situation in which people earn the same for a week spent producing trousers as they would for one spent producing shoes. Otherwise they would switch to the other trade. When incomes are more or less equalised over all productive activities, commodities are produced in the proportions that people wish to consume them. The total labour available to our village, or to any other society based on simple commodity production, is allocated between different trades in the proportions that the inhabitants desire.

If people change their preferences, opting for, say, more shoes and fewer trousers at £20 each, the demand for shoes rises and the price goes up. The demand for trousers falls, as does their price. Tailors switch to being cobblers until earnings for a week spent making either shoes or trousers are equalised again. More shoes are produced and fewer trousers. This corresponds to society's new pattern of wants.

As for the balance between materials and final goods, if an unusually large number of people decide to make shoes and there is no leather, this will force up the price of leather, just as the price of shoes was forced up when they were scarce. People producing, say, soap will then switch to the production of leather because they can earn more by doing so. The supply of leather will increase and the shortage disappear.

In this situation, prices will tend to reflect time spent on production. If the tailor's and cobbler's earnings for a week are the same, and in this time the tailor makes ten pairs of trousers and the cobbler ten pairs of shoes, the price of both must be the same. If shoes can be made in half the time it takes to produce trousers, the latter will be twice as expensive as the former.

The above analysis contains all the basic principles of the law of value - the mechanism by which a society based on commodity production, where each individual acts so as to maximise his or her own economic well-being without concern for others, ensures a rational allocation of human labour between different trades. There remain some qualifications to be added, but these are only qualifications. In its essentials, the operation of the law of value is no more complex than the example of the cobbler and tailor.

The Law of Value - II

In general the prices of commodities tend to be proportional to the time required to produce them, thus equalising earnings in all trades. But what about a lazy artisan? Suppose a cobbler puts in as many hours as his competitors but spends half his time scratching his head and taking tea breaks. The indignant voices of reason and fairness demand that he should not get away with it. And indeed he will not. If he turns out only half the number of shoes as the others, he will earn only half as much. It is no good his pointing out that it took him twice as long to make each pair. The customer is interested only in buying a certain quality of shoe as cheaply as possible. If the lazy cobbler's shoes are no better than the others, they will not fetch a higher price.

Commodities tend to exchange at prices which are proportionate to the time required to produce them only if that time is spent working averagely hard or, as Marx puts it, if the work is done with an *average intensity of labour.*

A similar argument applies to the techniques of production used. If one cobbler sews by hand while another uses a sewing machine, the second will produce more shoes in a week without working any harder than the first.

Commodities tend to exchange in proportion to the labour expended in their production only if that labour is of an average intensity and uses an *averagely efficient technique of production.*

Finally, skills must be taken into account. Within a trade, the argument follows the now familiar pattern. If a cobbler's sewing abilities are below average, he will, if he works averagely hard using an averagely efficient technique of production, produce less shoes in a week than his competitors.

The problem is complicated by the fact that some jobs require more skills than others. The village doctor, for example, needs a wider range of knowledge and techniques than the baker. Certain jobs require more training than others.[3]

The degree of skill can be measured in terms of the training involved. Suppose that an average working life is 30 years and that it takes 10 years' training to acquire the skills for a particular trade. There are 20 human years involved in training: 10 years of the trainee's working life and 10 years of the teacher's. The qualified worker can do the job for another 20 years. Therefore every year (or hour) of work actually involves two years (or hours) of human labour, because an equal amount of time to that spent doing the job is involved in acquiring the necessary skills. Each hour of skilled labour is equivalent to two hours of unskilled work. A commodity embodying one hour of skilled labour will therefore tend to fetch the same price as one embodying two hours of unskilled work.[4]

Marx calls unskilled labour *simple labour* - as opposed to complex or skilled labour - and labour worked averagely hard with the average technique of production *socially necessary labour*.

Commodities thus tend to exchange in proportion to the amount of socially necessary simple labour time required for their production. Marx calls simple, socially necessary labour time *value*. Commodities therefore tend to exchange in proportion to their values. Hence Marx's use of the expression the law of value as shorthand for the mechanism which allocates social labour between jobs in a society based on commodity production.

The relationship between actual labour performed and its equivalent in terms of value is very important to commodity producers. Suppose that the law of value has worked to allocate total social labour between trades in precisely the proportions that society desires. If tailoring and shoemaking are equally skilled trades, the income of the average tailor and cobbler will be the same. If the average output of both trades is four pairs of shoes or trousers per week then both will sell for the same price. Now suppose that a particular cobbler has only half as efficient a technique of production as the average, say he has no sewing machine and has to stitch by hand. Although he works just as hard as his competitors, he is only able to produce two pairs of shoes a week. His shoes sell at their value but, because the value created by his labour is only half the actual hours performed, his income is only half the average. This is of more than academic interest to him.

The value of shoes or trousers is not determined solely by the value created by the cobbler or tailor. The labour required to produce shoes includes that involved in killing the cow, tanning the hide, making the thread to sew the leather and so on. All the constituent elements of the final product contain value, which therefore has to be traced back like the house that Jack built.

The value created by labour engaged in producing the materials from which the commodity is made is transferred to the final product. It would be clear that the value of the work of tanning and so on is transferred to the shoes if one person performed all the operations, from killing the cow to hammering on soles. It is less apparent if the final producer starts with materials produced by someone else. But, from the point of view of society as a whole, the process is identical. It is the total labour required to produce shoes from beginning to end which determines their value. The cobbler *adds* value, by his labour of stitching, to that *transferred* from the materials on which he works.

The practical importance of this can be seen in the way labour is allocated and prices are determined. When the cobbler has sold all his shoes he has to spend some of his earnings on leather and thread to make the following week's batch. Only after he has replaced the materials used in making this week's shoes can he spend money on himself; on food, clothes and whatever else he needs. It is the money he can spend on himself that interests him. He would be no better off receiving £15 a week more for his shoes if the price of a week's worth of leather and thread rose by £15. When considering whether to switch jobs, he will want to know the tailor's earnings after replacement of the materials used to make trousers. If the cobbler earns £80 a week and spends £15 on leather and thread, he has £65 left for himself. If the tailor makes £85, but has to spend £20 on cloth, they are equally well off. The cobbler would gain nothing by becoming a tailor.

The effect of people switching jobs if they can earn more by doing so is to create a tendency for incomes to be equalised *after replacement of materials* used up in the work process. Thus commodities tend to exchange at rates proportional to their *total value*; that is, value transferred plus value added.

Account must also be taken of the labour engaged in producing tools. Value is transferred to a commodity from means of labour as well as its objects. But the value embodied in a needle is not transferred to a pair of shoes all at once. The same needle is used to make many pairs and so its value is only transferred slowly. If it can be used to sew 10 pairs of shoes, after which it is too blunt to be of further use, one tenth of its value is transferred to each pair of shoes.

Again it would be clear that value is transferred from means of labour to final products if the same person produced both. Suppose Robinson Crusoe needs to dig some holes. He has to decide whether to dig with his bare hands or to spend time making a spade. If it takes two hours to dig a hole by hand, and there are 10 holes to be dug, then, without a spade, the whole operation will take 20 hours. If a spade which will survive being used to dig 10 holes only can be produced in five hours, the whole operation can be carried out in only 15 hours. Overall, it will take Robinson an average of one and a half hours to dig each hole - one hour spent digging and half an hour spent making the spade.

In the village, artisans buy their means of labour. But from the point of view of society as a whole, the situation is identical to the one Crusoe faces. The quantity of value transferred from a tool to a final product is determined by the amount of socially necessary labour time required to produce the tool and the number of productive processes for which it can be used. If it takes five hours to produce a needle which can be used to make 20 pairs of shoes, a quarter of an hour of value is transferred to each pair.

Again this will show itself in the prices commodities fetch on the market. People will tend to switch jobs until the income received after regular replacement of materials and tools is the same in all trades. Commodities will tend to exchange at prices which are determined by their values; that is, the value added by the final producer to that transferred from both objects and means of labour.

$$
\left.
\begin{array}{l}
\text{value of leather, thread, etc, used} \\
+ \ \text{value of the part of tools 'used up'}
\end{array}
\right\} \quad \textit{value transferred}
$$

$$
+ \ \text{value added making shoes} \qquad \textit{value added}
$$

$$
\overline{}
$$

$$
= \ \text{value of pair of shoes}
$$

These, then, are the necessary qualifications to the earlier account of the operation of the law of value under simple commodity production. People tend to switch jobs if they can earn more for a week's work in another trade after taking account of the money that must be set aside to replace both materials and tools. This tends to produce a situation in which the prices of commodities are proportional to their values; that is, the equivalent in terms of simple socially necessary labour time of the actual time expended both directly and indirectly in their production. This, in turn, tends to produce a situation in which total social labour is allocated between trades, and hence different goods are produced, in the proportions that society as a whole desires.

Value, Exchange Value and Price

A commodity is both a use value and an exchange value. It has properties capable of satisfying a human want and is exchangeable on a market. The operation of the law of value under simple commodity production tends to produce a situation in which commodities exchange at rates proportional to their values. In short, the exchange value of a commodity tends to be determined by its value.

How is the exchange value of a commodity expressed? In what units can it be measured? One answer is *values*, hours of simple socially necessary labour time. Under this system, the exchange value of a product is measured by the amount of society's labour expended in the production of other goods which can be obtained in exchange for it. This is in an important sense the most meaningful way to express exchange value; in terms of the real cost involved in production, the expenditure of human effort.

But it is not possible in practice to express exchange value in terms of value. The socially necessary labour time required to produce something is never apparent. Even if the actual labour time is known, it is not possible to evaluate how much of it is socially necessary. If we cluster around a hole in a hoarding and watch builders at work, we cannot tell precisely how far their intensity of work, degree of skill and techniques of production differ from the averages in the industry. Commodities are not stamped with their values in hours, minutes and seconds.

An alternative is to express exchange value in terms of other commodities. One chair might be worth - that is, could be exchanged for - 2 pairs of shoes, 3 coats or 8 pounds of carrots. This is the way in which exchange value is expressed in barter economies, ones in which goods are literally swapped.

In more advanced commodity-producing societies, exchange values are expressed in *prices*, units of money such as pounds and pence. An account of the way in which money evolved historically lies outside the scope of this book. But it is important to note that the process was a social rather than a natural one. Money has not always existed and need not always do so in future.

Money functions as such because people are prepared to accept it in payment for commodities. Some authority may designate a substance as money by decree, as with state-issued bank notes, but people must be prepared to accept it in payment for that decree to have effect. If people become unwilling to accept state-issued currencies, they cease to act as money. When this happens some other substance is often spontaneously adopted to fulfil the functions of money. The most famous example is the use of cigarettes in Germany during the inflation of 1923.

Unlike values, prices are immediately visible. Commodities are often literally stamped with them, as in supermarkets. Money provides a uniform standard for measuring the exchange value of all commodities. A certain type of shoe costs £16 a pair, which is twice the exchange value of a shirt selling for £8 and four times that of a hat going for £4.

If the law of value succeeded in allocating labour between different trades in precisely the proportions that society desired, relative values, exchange values and prices would all be equal. If half as much socially necessary labour time was required to produce a coat as a pair of shoes, the value of the coat would be half that of the shoes, as would its exchange value and price.

But, while commodities of equal value tend to have equal exchange values and prices, they do not always do so. Indeed, the law of value could not operate if relative prices did not sometimes differ from relative values. Suppose that on one market day in the village labour is allocated between trades in precisely the proportions that the inhabitants desire. Trousers and shoes exchange in proportion to their values. But the following week people decide they prefer more trousers and fewer shoes. The price of trousers rises above their value and that of shoes falls below theirs. Cobblers earn less than tailors. Some switch trades. A new division of labour is established in accordance with the villagers' changed preferences. This process could not occur without prices rising above or falling below values in response to changes in the balance between the supply of and demand for particular goods.

It is impossible to establish at any given moment whether prices are proportional to values and hence whether labour is allocated between trades in precisely the proportions that society desires. But it would be a pure fluke if this situation were ever achieved, even momentarily. There are three main reasons why, even in a society based on a pure form of simple commodity production, the law of value is unlikely to achieve a perfect allocation of labour.

The first is that the balance of goods, and hence the proportional allocation of social labour, that society desires are constantly changing. Just as stallholders are beaming at each other from behind piles of cheese and bread, carefully calculated to meet the usual demand, a new craze starts. People go off cheese and onto cream buns. As soon as artisans begin switching trades in response to the new pattern of demand, tastes change again. Someone invents ice-cream.

Secondly, values change. New techniques of production are discovered which reduce the socially necessary labour time required to produce particular commodities and thereby alter the proportional allocation of labour needed to achieve a given pattern of output. If a sewing machine is invented which reduces the time required to make trousers, fewer tailors are needed.

The law of value can never keep completely abreast of these changes. It works to try and achieve a desired allocation of social labour, which is itself constantly changing.

Finally, even if tastes and values remained the same, there is no guarantee that the law of value would achieve precisely the division of labour desired. There is no mechanism to ensure that when people switch jobs, the *right number* do so. Suppose society's preferences change so that 10 per cent fewer trousers and 10 per cent more shoes are required. The price of trousers falls and that of shoes rises. Tailors earn less than cobblers. Each tailor must make a decision about whether to change trades by guessing how many others will do so. There is no reason to suppose that exactly the right number will become cobblers. Meanwhile, the number required to do so is constantly changing as tastes and values alter.

Why study the law of value if it works so imperfectly? Because, although imperfect, it *does* work. Economic systems which are not consciously directed require a regulating mechanism. Social labour must be allocated between trades in proportions which, although never perfect, are good enough to prevent permanent and chronic shortages occurring. Societies based on various forms of commodity production have existed for long periods of time and it is the operation of the law of value, albeit imperfect, which has sustained them.

3. Artisanal Production and Bourgeois Socialism

How do people relate to each other in economic activity under simple commodity production? On what *social relations* is it based?

When analysing the social relations of any economic system, Marx distinguished two aspects, or levels, of the overall process of expending effort to satisfy human needs. One is that of the labour process, the actual process of transforming nature to produce use values. Marx called this the level of *the appropriation of nature* or that of *production*. It includes only the labour process itself. The social relations here are those of the work place.

The other aspect of economic activity is the distribution of use values: the process whereby elements of production and products pass from producers or owners to the people who use them. Marx calls this the level of *the appropriation of the product* or that of *circulation*. Social relations here include all economic relations between people outside of the labour process.

In the model of simple commodity production outlined in the two previous sections, no social relations exist at the level of production. The labour process is an individual interaction between each artisan and nature. The baker works on his own kneading dough to bake bread. The blacksmith hammers at his anvil alone.

Because there are no social relations within production there can be no question of inequality or of the coercion of some people by others in the labour process. Each artisan has control over the elements of production and can choose the manner and pace of work.

Of course, there are pressures on all artisans to work efficiently. If they are lazy or use a relatively inefficient technique, they will earn less than their competitors because the value they produce in a week will be lower. But these constraints are imposed by the operation of the law of value via the market; that is, by the social relations of circulation. They do not result from coercive relationships between people within production itself. No one stands over simple commodity producers telling them to work harder or in a different way.

Many ways of organising production do involve social relations at the level of production, often of an unequal and coercive nature. Under slavery, for example, the dominant relationship between people in the labour process is that between slavemaster and slaves. The slavemaster is in a position of authority and control. He stands over the slaves with a whip, telling them how to work and how hard to work.

In our model of simple commodity production, social relations exist only in circulation. People relate to each other in exchange. They meet at the market to buy and sell commodities. The nature and significance of these relationships are discussed in detail below (chapter 4). For the moment, the important thing is that they are relations of freedom and equality. Everyone is in turn both a seller and a buyer. Whether buying or selling, no one is compelled to do so from or to a particular person or at a particular price.

Of course, if anyone charges too much for their goods, no

one will buy from them. Similarly, if they are not prepared to pay enough, no one will sell to them. But the prices that prevail are not fixed by anyone in a position of authority or control. The only coercion that exists is the economic pressure of market forces, regulated by the law of value. This tends not only to affect everyone equally, but also to allocate labour to the production of different goods in more or less the proportions society desires and to ensure that a similar income is received for a week's work in all trades. In short, it tends to produce an equitable outcome.

Simple commodity production, then, is a logically possible way of organising economic activity on the basis of free and equal relationships between people.

No society organised in this way has ever existed. Of course, economic activity seldom, if ever, takes place in exact accordance with the principles of a model. Societies frequently include several economic systems. In Britain today, for example, whilst production is predominantly organised along capitalist lines other forms of economic activity nevertheless take place, including artisanal production by the self-employed. The operation of the principle economic system in a society also invariably differs in detail from that of a model. Complications and distortions are always present in actual historical situations. The purpose of a model is to abstract from inessential complications and thereby illuminate the basic features of a system. But simple commodity production is even further distanced from historical reality.

Production by artisans did take place on a significant scale during the period of transition from natural economy to fully fledged commodity production. But it never became the dominant form of economic activity. At first, it existed under the wings of feudalism. By the time production for sale became general artisanal activity had been eclipsed by the rise of capitalism. Moreover, even in its heyday, artisanal production involved unequal, hierarchical and coercive social relations.

At the level of production, the basic unit of the system was the family rather than the individual. Within the family, the father often played a hierarchical and coercive role. He would tell his wife and children how to work and how hard to work. It is no coincidence that all the artisans in the earlier examples were male.

Because people had to learn trades, apprenticeships were common. Thus artisans were also frequently in a position of authority and control over apprentices. This authority was often enforced with violence.

Similar inequalities existed in circulation. In the model, it was assumed that people could switch jobs at the drop of a price. In practice it was never this easy. Two important obstacles were skills and means of production. To change jobs, an artisan had to learn a new trade and obtain the necessary means of production. Skills were generally acquired slowly, by a long apprenticeship, and means of production inherited. As a result, the law of value worked very imperfectly. There could be and were persistent inequalities of income between trades.

One way for an artisan to obtain new means of production was to borrow money. This was the basis for an important inequality in circulation: usury or *money-lending*. By charging interest on loans, money-lenders acquired enough to live on - and often a great deal more - without working. By owning money, they were able to control the ownership of an element of production: artisans could obtain new means of production only by going into debt to a money-lender. Money-lenders therefore constituted an exploiting class, able to extract a tribute from the artisans.

Another factor bringing about inequality and coercion in circulation was the existence of trade monopolies. If a group had control over essential objects of labour, such as raw cotton imported from abroad, then artisans needing that commodity were forced to buy from this group. Since the group did not face any competition, it could change a price in excess of the commodity's value. Since the artisans were dependent on the group for an essential object of labour, they could be forced to sell the finished goods back to the group, this time at a price below value. Finally, since the group faced no competition on the market, the finished goods could be sold to consumers above their value.

By having such a monopoly, a group could dictate who the artisans bought from and sold to and the prices at which they did so. By selling commodities above their value and buying them below it, those who maintained the monopoly could make a profit. Like the money-lenders, they constituted an exploiting class which, by controlling one of the elements of production - usually an object of labour - could extract a tribute. Marx called the members of this class *merchant capitalists*.

The main elements of Proudhon's programme were reforms designed to abolish elements of coercion and inequality found in artisanal production. One of his central demands was for free credit. The state was to provide interest-free loans to all who needed them. This reform would have done away with usury and abolished the money-lenders as a class. It would also have made it easier to change trades, thus assisting the operation of the law of value.

The abolition of trade monopolies - also central to Proudhon's programme - would have eliminated the main basis for merchant capital. It would have abolished one of the major unequal and coercive relations between people and again facilitated the operation of the law of value.

Some of the proudhonists' other proposals were completely misguided, such as their plan to abolish money which they believed responsible for many of the distortions afflicting an essentially equitable society. They planned to replace money with *labour time chits* - pieces of paper representing a certain number of hours' work. Under this system, someone who had worked for six hours would be given a piece of paper 'worth' six hours' labour which could then be exchanged for commodities whose production had taken six hours. This particular scheme, far from making simple commodity production work more smoothly, would have hindered the operation of the law of value because it did not differentiate between actual and socially necessary labour time. It would, for example, have allowed a lazy baker to earn as much as his hardworking competitors because differences in intensity of labour would no longer be recognised on the market.

In addition, the bourgeois socialists failed to recognise

certain important instances of inequality. They were generally blind to those within production as opposed to circulation. For example, they appear to have had no conception of hierarchical relationships within the family and hence to have put forward no proposals designed to prevent male artisans from coercing their wives and children.

But these weaknesses were not crucial. It would have been possible to replace erroneous proposals with sound ones in the spirit of the proudhonists' intentions and to extend their programme to cover omissions. If the spread of exchange relations were leading to a generalisation of artisanal production which would become, and henceforth remain, the basic way of organising production - as eternal and immutable as the solar system - then this approach would have been correct.

But this was not happening. Commodity exchange had given birth to capitalism. Proudhon failed to appreciate the profound effects this had on the development of the productive forces, ruling out a return to artisanal production and laying the basis for a free and equal society organised on different principles to those of commodity production (see chapter 5). Equally importantly he misunderstood the nature of capitalist social relations, the subject of the next chapter.

3. Exploitation and Surplus Value

This chapter examines capitalism. How does it differ from simple commodity production? Is it based on essentially free and equal social relations or does it necessarily involve inequality and coercion?

This last question is politically crucial. Bourgeois socialism is concerned with eradicating frictions in the workings of a system based on commodity production. It is a viable approach to creating an egalitarian community if, and only if, the system to which it is applied is capable of functioning without inequality and coercion. Is capitalism such a system?

1. The Social Relations of Capitalism

Circulation under Capitalism

In circulation, the only major difference between simple commodity production and capitalism is that under capitalism an extra commodity appears on the market. This is workers' capacity for labour. Under simple commodity production, artisans own means of labour, work on their own account and sell products. Their ability to work is not offered for sale. Capitalism - based on wage labour - involves workers selling their capacity for work, rather than products. Marx calls the capacity to work *labour power*.

Labour power is not labour. Marx uses the following analogy to explain the distinction. Just as the human body is permanently capable of digesting food, though the process of digestion takes place only when food is consumed, so labour power is the capacity to work while labour is the actual process of working.

One of Marx's definitions of capitalism is based on this difference between simple commodity production and capitalism at the level of circulation. Capitalism is, he says, commodity production generalised to include labour power as a commodity.

What determines the value and price of this new commodity, labour power? The value of any commodity is the socially necessary labour time required to produce it. What is the labour time required to produce labour power? It is the time required to produce workers' means of subsistence: the commodities they need to consume to replace the brain, nerves and muscles used up in the process of working. The means of subsistence are the goods and services needed to make good the mental and physical wear and tear that constitute the real human costs of production.

Means of subsistence should not be thought of too narrowly. They include more than minimum physiological requirements for survival. For one thing they include goods needed to bring up future generations of workers. Their upbringing is primarily the responsibility of their parents, whose means of subsistence must therefore include enough to support children if capitalism is to exist for more than one generation.

But means of subsistence include more than minimum requirements for the physical survival of workers and their dependents. Workers must do more than survive: they must turn up to work each morning. Imagine the reaction if Henry Ford did a little research and then held a meeting of his workforce, saying 'Look I've worked it out. You only need a certain calorie intake, so much clothing and heating and a house of a certain standard. You can buy all that for £20 a week, so I've decided that's all I'm going to pay you from now on'!

Means of subsistence include goods which, while not physiologically essential, have become a normal part of day to day life. Marx called these the *customary and historical element* in the value of labour power. This varies at different times in history and in different places and cultures. Nowadays, beer and cigarettes are as much a part of the means of subsistence as are bread and potatoes.

Given the components of the means of subsistence, the value of labour power depends on the time required to produce them - on their value. This depends primarily on the level of development of the productive forces, the ease with and extent to which human beings are able to transform nature.

The price of labour power is, like the price of all commodities, its exchange value expressed in terms of money. It is the amount of money which must be paid to buy it. Just as the price of a loaf of bread is the sum of money which will persuade a baker to sell a loaf, the price of labour power is the sum a capitalist must pay in wages to persuade people to work in his factory.

Since the value of labour power is the value of means of subsistence, you would expect its exchange value to be the same as that of means of subsistence. In other words, you would expect the wage to be equal to the price of the means of subsistence, so that workers earned exactly enough to buy them. In general this is so.

But while prices tend to equal values they do not always do so. Prices must be able to differ from values for the law of value to operate. When the supply of a commodity gets out of line with the demand for it because society desires a different proportion of total social labour to be employed in its production, its price deviates from its value. If society desires more of that commodity and less of others, its price rises above its value. People become attracted into its production and the supply is increased. Price then falls back down to value.

The price of labour power can deviate from its value in a similar way. If capitalists require more workers than are currently available, they may bid wages above the value of labour power. Similarly, if more people are looking for work than capitalists wish to employ, wages may fall below the value of labour power.

But a difference exists between labour power and other commodities. Commodity producers - artisans or capitalists - cannot move into the production of labour power. Whilst our tailor might decide to become a worker if wages rose, he could not move into the production of workers, for they are hardly produced in the same way as coats.[1] This is important in relation to the development of capitalism over time (see chapter 6).

The social relations of circulation under capitalism, as under simple commodity production, are ones of freedom and equality. Everyone is equal before the market. Workers buy means of subsistence there; capitalists buy labour power, machines and materials. No one forces anybody else to buy from particular people or at a particular price. No non-economic coercion exists.

Everyone is also a seller on the market. Workers sell their ability to labour and capitalists sell products. Again, there is no non-economic coercion. Nobody is forced to sell at a particular price or to particular people. No fraud is involved.

The flowers of freedom and equality bloom. Any pests in the foliage, such as merchant capitalists or money-lenders, are no more essential to capitalism than to simple commodity production. No unequal or coercive social relations fundamental to the system have yet come to light. Proudhonism appears to be a viable perspective. So far.

Production under Capitalism

What happens to commodities once they leave the sphere of circulation? What happens after free and equal exchange has taken place?

Once someone has bought a pair of shoes, a tin of beans or a loaf of bread, they can do as they like with them. If they choose to cut the shoes to pieces, pile the tins into models of the Eiffel Tower or use the bread as wallpaper, no one can legitimately object. They own the shoes, the tins, the bread. They have paid the going price and the goods are theirs, to consume however they wish.

Apply the same logic to a capitalist's purchase of labour power. Once he has bought it, he owns it, just as he owns machinery and materials. He has paid the market price for it, determined in general by its value. It is his to use as he wishes.

How will he use it? The answer is obvious. He will put it to work. He has bought the capacity to work because he intends to activate it: to put labourers to work in his factory producing commodities.

Although capitalism and simple commodity production are essentially similar at the level of circulation, they differ fundamentally at the level of production. In the pure model of simple commodity production, there are no social relations involved in the transformation of nature. There are under capitalism. Capitalists and workers do not only enter into economic relations with each other on the market. They continue relating after exchange has taken place. These social relations are not ones of freedom and equality. On the contrary, they are hierarchical and coercive. The capitalist no longer confronts the workers as an equal, as in the market place, but as a superior. He is in a position of authority and control. Because he has bought workers' labour power, he is able to tell them how to work and how hard to work. He runs the show.

Marx humorously contrasts the freedom and equality of circulation with the inequality and coercion of production:

> The sphere of circulation or commodity exchange, within whose boundaries the sale and purchase of labour power goes on, is in fact a very Eden of the innate rights of man. It is the exclusive realm of Freedom (and) Equality ... Freedom, because both buyer and seller of a commodity, let us say of labour power, are determined only by their own free will. They contract as free persons, who are equal before the law. Their contract is the final result in which their joint will finds a common legal expression. Equality, because each enters into relation with the other, as with a simple owner of commodities, and they exchange equivalent for equivalent ... When we leave this sphere of simple circulation or the exchange of commodities ... a certain change takes place, or so it appears, in the physiognomy of our *dramatis personae*. He who was previously the money owner now strides out in front as capitalist; the possessor of labour power follows as his worker. The one smirks self-importantly and is intent on business; the other is timid and holds back, like someone who has brought his own hide to market and now has nothing else to expect but a tanning.[2]

Here, then, is the inequality and coercion fundamental to

capitalism. It occurs inside the factory gate, behind the sign that reads: 'No Admittance Except On Business'. It is located at the point of production, within the labour process itself.

2. How Capitalism Works

The Origin of Profit

Under simple commodity production, artisans buy means and objects of labour at prices determined, in general, by their values. They then work with these to produce commodities which they sell. The prices they receive for their products are again, in general, determined by their values. The difference between the value transferred from means and objects of labour to the product and its total value is that which they add by their work. This additional value yields them an income.

Under capitalism, capitalists buy objects of labour, means of labour and labour power. The price of these is again determined, in general, by their values. They set the labour power to work with the means and objects of labour to produce commodities, which they sell. The prices they receive for the products are again determined, in general, by their values.

How do capitalists gain from this process? Like artisans, they buy and sell everything at value. But, unlike artisans, they themselves do not work. The work is done by people whose labour power they have bought. Capitalists do not personally add value. How do they emerge from the process owning more than they began with? Why are they able to sell the products for more than they had to pay to buy machines and materials and to hire workers? How do capitalists make a *profit*?

The answer is that one commodity they buy has a special property. The commodity is labour power and the property it has, which no other commodity possesses, is that *it is capable of creating value*. Value is human labour time, adjusted for intensity, skill etc. Labour power is the capacity for work. When that capacity is activated it produces value. The value it creates is embodied in the commodities workers produce. The total value of the product is, as in simple commodity production, the value transferred from objects and means of labour plus that added in the process of using these to make products.

Like the artisan, the capitalist in general buys means and objects of labour at their values. This value forms part of the price of the product. Unlike the artisan, he also buys labour power. Whether he receives more for his products than he has to pay for their production clearly depends on whether the value created by the workers he hires exceeds that of their labour power. Because workers are *capable* of producing more value than that of their labour power it is *possible* for capitalists to make a profit. It is possible, but not inevitable.

After all, it is not in workers' interests to work harder than they have to. The capitalist has to compel them to produce more value than that of their labour power. If he does not, he makes no profit and goes out of business. He is able to force the production of extra value by exercising authority and control over his workforce. He does so by virtue of the unequal and coercive social relations that exist within the labour process under capitalism. Marx calls the process whereby capitalists force workers to create more value than that of their labour power *exploitation*.

He calls the means and objects of labour *constant capital* and labour power - workers themselves - *variable capital*. Calling workers as well as machines *capital* emphasises that once the worker has sold his capacity for work it belongs to the capitalist, just as do machines. Means and objects of labour are *constant* capital because the value they impart to the product is fixed. Machines and materials simply transfer their value to the product. Workers, on the other hand, are *variable* capital because the amount of value they impart to the product is not fixed in the same way. They create value rather than simply transferring that of their labour power. How much value they create depends on how effectively capitalists can exploit them.

The labour performed and value created by workers each consists of two parts. One is labour required to produce the means of subsistence. Marx calls this *necessary labour*. The value it creates is equal to that of labour power purchased. The extra work put in is surplus labour. This creates *surplus value.*

This division would be obvious if workers produced one commodity only, with which they were also paid. Imagine an economy in which only potatoes are produced. Workers plant, tend and harvest potatoes and are paid their 'wages' in potatoes. With 10 pounds of potatoes to use as seed and a worker who can be forced to perform 40 hours' work, a capitalist can obtain a crop of 50 pounds of potatoes. 40 hours of work produce 40 extra pounds of potatoes, since the capitalist starts with 10 pounds and ends up with 50. The value of each pound is therefore one hour. The total value of the product is 50 hours, of which 10 are transferred from the seed potatoes and 40 added by the worker. If the wage for 40 hours' work is 20 pounds of potatoes, it is clear that 20 hours represent necessary labour, required to produce means of subsistence. The other 20 hours are surplus labour, producing surplus value. These 20 hours yield the capitalist his profit of 20 pounds of potatoes.

Suppose potatoes cost £1 per pound. The capitalist pays £10 for seed potatoes and £20 in wages. He sells the crop for £50 and makes £20 profit. The worker is able to buy half of the extra potatoes he produced. It is still clear that half the labour performed is surplus labour, creating surplus value and yielding the capitalist his profit.[3]

In the real world, in which a wide range of goods is produced and consumed, it is more difficult to establish the surplus value produced by a single worker. It is necessary to look instead at the time put in by all workers, at total social labour.

The total output produced embodies a certain value. A part of this is value transferred from means and objects of labour, so that some of the *gross output* must be used to replace machines and materials if society's productive potential is to be maintained. The remainder is *net output.* This embodies the value added by workers. Part of it consists of workers' means of subsistence. The time taken to produce these is necessary labour. Their value is the value of labour power. The rest is surplus product. The time taken to produce this is surplus labour. Its value is the surplus value which workers have been forced to produce.

This division is summarised in the diagram below. The total (t) is the value of the gross output that capitalists have compelled workers to produce over a certain period. Part of this is value transferred from constant capital (c). This represents the value of means and objects of labour used up in producing t. Net output ($v + s$) is value added to c. It is the labour performed and value added by workers during production. Part of it (v) is the value of labour power, that required to maintain variable capital. The rest is surplus value (s). The numbers in brackets are taken from the example of an imaginary potato economy.

$$t \quad = \quad c \quad + \quad v \quad + \quad s$$
$$(50) \quad (10) \quad (20) \quad (20)$$

Exploitation, then, is the process whereby the capitalist class forces the working class to perform more labour than that required to produce its means of subsistence. The surplus labour that workers are compelled to perform produces surplus value. This is embodied in commodities. Capitalists make a profit by selling these commodities. The amount of profit they make is the sum of the prices of all those commodities produced during surplus labour time and hence embodying surplus value. *Surplus labour, producing surplus value, is the source of profit.*

The *rate of exploitation* is the ratio between surplus and necessary labour. It is surplus value divided by the value of labour power: s/v. It is also known as the rate of surplus value. In the example of the potato economy the rate of exploitation is 20/20 or 100 per cent.

The *rate of profit* is the ratio between the profit the capitalist makes - revenue from selling final products minus the costs of producing them - and the money he has to pay out to get production going. In the potato economy this is $s/c + v = 20/30$, or just under 67 per cent.

But the rate of profit is not always the ratio between profit and costs. Suppose a tractor is used to harvest potatoes. It costs £100 and lasts for 10 years. The cost of producing one year's crop is now £40 - £20 wages, £10 seed potatoes and £10 worth of tractor. But the money the capitalist has tied up in the first year is

£130 - £100 for the tractor, £20 wages and £10 for seed potatoes. The rate of profit in that year is not 20/30 but 20/130, or just over 15 per cent. The rate of profit is thus profit divided by total capital (k), or $s/k + v$. k exceeds c if any means of production last longer than a single production process.

The rate of profit and the rate of surplus value are both ways of expressing the relation between surplus and the cost of producing it. But they differ in two important ways. One is the units in which they measure both surplus and costs. The rate of profit is measured in money terms, the rate of surplus value in units of value. They also differ as to what they consider as costs. The rate of surplus value counts as costs only the value of means of subsistence while the rate of profit counts all the money the capitalist has tied up in elements of production.

These two different ways of expressing the relationship between the surplus and its cost of production reflect different class perspectives. The rate of profit expresses the rate of return a capitalist obtains for using money as capital. He begins with a sum of money with which he buys elements of production. He sets these to work to produce commodities which he then sells. He begins and ends the process with money. The rate of profit is the measure of the proportion by which his money grows.

The rate of surplus value, on the other hand, measures the extent to which workers are forced to produce value over and above that of their labour power. They are compelled to perform a certain amount of work. In return for this they receive a wage which allows them to buy means of subsistence. These are only a part of the total volume of commodities produced. Workers receive only a part of the value they create. The rate of surplus value measures how much of the work they perform is necessary from their point of view, how much is required to produce the goods they consume. It is the quantitative expression of the extent to which they are exploited by capitalists.

Diagram 2 (p. 62) summarises the processes of exchange under simple commodity production and capitalism. Under the former, artisans go to market with commodities (c) they have produced. They sell these for money (m) which they then spend on

Diagram 2

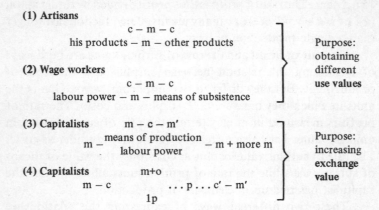

other commodities (c). They begin and end the process with commodities. The total prices of both sets of commodities are the same but the goods are qualitatively different. The purpose of exchange is the acquisition of different use values.

Take our old friend the tailor. He arrives at the market with trousers to sell. He spends the money he gets for them on cloth, needles and thread to make more trousers and on food, tobacco and the like for himself. Money has been nothing more than a means of exchanging one set of goods for another. It has not stayed in his pocket long enough to wear a hole.

For workers under capitalism, the process, though similar, does not begin with products they have made because these always belong to the capitalists for whom they work. Workers do not own means of production and so cannot work on their own account. Nevertheless, they do own a commodity. They sell their labour power and spend the wage on means of subsistence. The exchange values of their labour power and of the means of subsistence are the same. Again, money is only a means to an end. The point of the exercise is, as under simple commodity production, the acquisition of different use values.

The process is altogether different for a capitalist. It begins and ends with money. There is no qualitative change, only a quantitative one. He finishes up with more money than he began with (m' instead of m). The purpose is not the acquisition of different use values, but an increase in the amount of exchange value under his control. Means and ends are reversed for him.

The secret of how, unlike artisans and workers, the capitalist finishes up with more exchange value than he began with lies in the fact that the exchanges he makes are separated (...) by the process of production (p). The capitalist spends his initial money capital on means and objects of labour (m + o) and labour power (lp). He then sets the labour power to work and, using his position of authority and control in the labour process, forces workers to perform surplus labour. The commodities they produce embody more value than those he bought and therefore sell for more money. The capitalist makes a profit. This is summarised in the fourth part of diagram 2.

This profit has not been made in exchange - where everything has been bought and sold at value - but in production, where exploitation has taken place. Marx said of his analysis of the source of profit:

> I furthermore show in detail that even in the exchange of commodities, only equivalents are exchanged, the capitalist - as soon as he paid the worker the actual value of his labour power - proceeded to acquire the *surplus value* with all the right in the world, that is, with the right that corresponds to this mode of production.[4]

Exploitation is not an aberration from free and equal commodity exchange. It is rather the logical and, within its own terms, rightful product of it once labour power becomes a commodity. It is fully consistent with both the letter and spirit of the rules of exchange and therefore cannot be abolished by an appeal to, or tinkering with, those rules.

The Operation of the Law of Value under Capitalism

Capitalism, like simple commodity production, lacks central direction or planning. Each capitalist decides on the type and quantity of products to produce. Each worker decides which commodities to spend his wage on. Thus the same problem arises as with simple commodity production: how is labour allocated in proportions which ensure that a workable balance between the production of cornflakes, hairsprays and other commodities is achieved?

The mechanism is once again the law of value. This works in essentially the same way under capitalism as under simple commodity production.

Capitalists are in business for profit. They are interested in the exchange value of their products in relation to the costs of producing them, not in their use values. They will therefore switch to producing other commodities if by doing so they can make more profit.

If one type of commodity is in relatively short supply, its price will rise. Capitalists producing it will make more profit than usual. Other capitalists will tend to move into its production because profits here are higher than average. This will increase supply and reduce price. Conversely, if a commodity is relatively over-supplied in relation to society's wants, its production will yield below average profits. Capitalists will tend to move out of its production, reducing supply and increasing price.

Changes in the allocation of social labour are brought about in this way. If capitalists decide to produce fewer cars, there is less demand for car workers. Some are sacked. If capitalists decide to produce more shoes, more jobs become available in shoemaking. Some workers are compelled to move out of the motor industry and into shoemaking if they are to find employment.

As under simple commodity production, individuals - both capitalists and workers - switch from one line of production to another on the basis of economic self-interest. This tends to produce a situation in which goods are produced in the relative proportions that society as a whole desires.

This tendency will never work itself out perfectly. As under simple commodity production, tastes and production techniques change and the mechanism suffers from imperfections. Nevertheless, it works sufficiently well to prevent chronic and permanent shortages.

Under simple commodity production, the operation of the law of value - the mechanism which allocates labour to the production of different goods - tends to bring about a situation in which relative prices are directly proportional to values. Under capitalism, however, the tendency is towards an equal rate of profit - revenues minus costs expressed as a proportion of money tied up in production - in all industries, since this is the only situation in which capitalists have no incentive to switch to the production of other commodities.

As more expensive means of production are required to produce some commodities than others, the proportions of money tied up in plant and machinery and in labour power differ between industries. Thus the prices of commodities involving outlays on plant and machinery larger than average in relation to labour power tend to be relatively higher than their values so as to yield the average rate of profit on capital employed. Conversely, the prices of commodities which involve a low expenditure on means of production in relation to labour power tend to be relatively lower than their values.

A simple example may serve to illustrate the point. Consider two capitalists in different industries. Both employ 10 workers at a weekly wage of £50 each and both use £100 worth of materials per week. One uses machinery costing £10,000 which lasts for 100 weeks, the other machinery costing £1000 and lasting for 10 weeks only. The prices of labour power, materials and machinery are directly proportional to their values - £1 purchasing one half hour of embodied labour. The rate of exploitation is 100 per cent. The value of gross weekly output is 600 hours in each firm (50 transferred from machinery, 50 transferred from materials and 500 added). 250 hours' surplus value is produced in each case. If output prices were directly proportional to values, both capitalists would make £500 profit per week. But this would mean very different *rates* of profit. For these to be equal, the price of the product requiring the more expensive machinery in its production must exceed that of the other.

Marx calls the exchange rates between commodities which the operation of the law of value tends to establish under capitalism *prices of production*. These are the relative prices which yield an equal rate of profit in all industries.

Because some commodities sell below their value and others sell above theirs, the profit each capitalist appropriates is not directly proportional to the surplus value his workers produce. Thus the divergence between prices of production and values influences the division of the spoils between the exploiters.

But the fact that commodities tend to exchange at prices of production rather than values does not invalidate any important element in the account of capitalism given so far. The assumption that prices of commodities tend to be proportional to values was made to simplify the exposition and to facilitate the comparison with simple commodity production. A few minutes' reflection should reassure anyone that a divergence between prices of production and values is irrelevant to the basic nature of the social relations of both circulation and production and to the origin of profit. No important political implications follow from it.

The Reproduction of the System

How are the conditions for undertaking production re-established after one batch of commodities is completed? How is it that all the elements needed for a repeat performance are available, and what ensures that they will be employed within capitalist social relations?

There are two sides to this question. One is the reproduction of use values. The right balance of consumer goods and of means and objects of labour must be produced if the system is to function. This is ensured by the operation of the law of value. If there have been no shortages in the last period, the rate of profit will have been equal in all sectors and there will be no incentive for any capitalist to switch to the production of different goods. If there have been shortages, the capitalist producing these goods will have received a higher than average rate of profit. Other capitalists will be attracted into these industries and the supply of these goods thereby increased.

The other side of the process of reproduction is the maintenance of capitalist social relations. The regular production of steel, baked beans and machine tools in workable proportions is not in itself the reproduction of capitalism, which is a particular way of organising production. If it is to continue, a specific set of social relations must be reproduced. After each period of production, there must be workers willing and able to re-sell their labour power and capitalists willing and able to buy it.

Viewed from the perspectives of individual workers and capitalists, it is not difficult to see how this is achieved. A worker is able to re-sell his labour power because he was paid for it last time around. He received a wage. This enabled him to buy means of subsistence to replace the brain, nerves and muscles used up in working (and to maintain his dependents). He was paid enough to keep him fit for work.

He began the last round of production owning the commodity labour power (c). He exchanged this for money (m) which he used to buy means of subsistence (c). By consuming these he made good the wear and tear that his labour power had undergone in the process of production.

A worker is willing to resell his capacity for work because he has no other option. There is no other way in which he can earn a living. He remains separated from the means of production. Capitalists still own the factories and so a worker has no choice but to work for them again.

A capitalist is able to hire workers, and to buy means and objects of labour for them to work with, because he has money in his hands. He began the last period of production with a sum of money (m) which he used to buy machines, materials and labour power $c \genfrac{}{}{0pt}{}{m+o}{1p}$. He set these to work to produce other commodities (c), which he sold. He ended the process as he began it. With money. He can use this to buy elements of production again, so that the process can continue.

$$m - c \quad \genfrac{}{}{0pt}{}{m+o}{1p} \quad \ldots c - m - c \quad \genfrac{}{}{0pt}{}{m+o}{1p} \quad \ldots c - m - c \quad \genfrac{}{}{0pt}{}{m+o}{1p} \quad \ldots$$

A capitalist is willing to re-hire workers because he can make a profit by doing so. He can force the workers to produce more value than that of their labour power. Thus he can sell the commodities workers produce for more than their cost of production and thereby increase his money capital. This provides the incentive for production.

There are, however, a number of important sides to reproduction which remain hidden if it is viewed only from the perspectives of individual workers and capitalists. These aspects become clear once the process is examined from the viewpoint of the system as a whole.

The money a capitalist has available grows period by period. He appropriates surplus value as profit. This is why he undertakes production. It is not a hobby for him, like some grander version of making model aeroplanes. He is in it for the money.

How will he use this extra money? Looked at from the point of view of an individual capitalist, it seems a matter of indifference. He could use it as additional capital, to make more profit. He could save it to provide for his old age. Finally, he could spend it on his own enjoyment, buying sports cars, yachts and so on. It would seem to be matter of personal preference, depending on whether he is inclined towards frugality or hedonism.

From the viewpoint of the system as a whole this is not so. If all capitalists were to try to save their profits, severe problems would result. At the end of a particular week, say, capitalists would attempt to sell their commodities. Those who had produced means of subsistence would find no difficulty. Workers would spend their wages on these and capitalists producing them would receive the usual rate of profit. But capitalists who had produced machines or luxury goods beyond workers means would be unable to sell these because other capitalists - their only potential customers - had decided not to spend their profits.

This situation is different to that of the overproduction of specific goods encountered earlier. There, a smaller than usual demand for trousers, say, was balanced by a greater than normal demand for some other commodity, such as shoes. The problem was one of the *proportions* between the supply of and demand for *particular* commodities. The law of value could work to correct this.

Here the problem is one of an imbalance between the supply of and demand for commodities *as a whole*. Capitalists are not attempting to spend their profits on goods other than the particular luxuries and means of labour produced. They have decided to save their money rather than buy anything at all. The normal operation of the law of value cannot solve this difficulty. If all capitalists move into the production of means of subsistence, for example, because these can apparently still be sold at a profit, overproduction occurs here. Workers' incomes - and hence demand - remain the same, whereas supply increases. Goods remain unsold or, if prices fall sufficiently to allow all goods to be sold, no profits are made. Capitalists' total revenues cannot exceed their wage costs in this situation because workers' wages are the only source of expenditure. Thus capitalists as a whole cannot make profits.

Ways in which difficulties of this kind may occur are discussed below (chapter 6). For the moment, the important point is that the reproduction of the system requires capitalists to spend their profits.

If capitalists are to make profits, they must be able both to force workers to produce a surplus product *and to sell it*. To use Marx's terminology, surplus value must be both produced and *realised*. Workers' wages allow them to buy the means of subsistence. Thus workers' expenditure is sufficient to realise the value embodied in means of subsistence, the value of labour power. *Surplus value must be realised by capitalists*. Thus the capitalist class can only make profits so long as it also spends them. If capitalists do not spend their profits - buying goods from each other - the surplus product cannot be sold, surplus value cannot be realised and so profits cannot be made.

Fortunately for the system, capitalists are compelled to

spend most of their profits on acquiring more elements of production. Capitalism is competitive. If one capitalist decides to save for his old age while his competitors use their profits as additional capital, he will get into trouble. His rivals will acquire more modern machines and be able to produce goods more cheaply. The commodities his workers produce will embody more labour time than those sold by his competitors, more than is socially necessary. So, although our capitalist's workforce will continue to put in as much *actual* labour time as before, it will produce less and less *value*. Less and less surplus value will be produced in our capitalist's firm. His profits will suffer and he will be driven out of business. To survive, a capitalist must act frugally and use profits to expand his capital.

So capitalist reproduction normally takes place on an expanded scale. It involves the use of previously produced surplus value, or profit, as additional capital. Reproduction takes place by means of the *accumulation* of capital. The ongoing cycle of production and exchange tends to expand continually. The last diagram should really have read:

$$m - c \quad \genfrac{}{}{0pt}{}{m+o}{1p} \quad \ldots c' - m' - c' \quad \genfrac{}{}{0pt}{}{m+o}{1p} \quad \ldots c'' -.m''$$

Where m′ is greater than m, c′ is greater than c, m″ is greater than m′ etc.

Since capitalists must consume something to survive, all capital is, after a time, previously produced surplus value. A simple example may clarify this. Suppose someone sets up in business with £1000 saved during 20 years of work as an artisan. The rate of profit is 15 per cent and it costs our new capitalist £50 to live during the time it takes his workers to produce commodities, say one week. After the first week he has £1150 (£1000 original capital plus £150 profit). He keeps back £50 living expenses for the next week and uses £1100 as capital. After 20 weeks he has spent all the £1000 he began with on day to day living. But he is not broke. He is considerably better off than when he started. His capital has expanded to over £11,000. All of this is surplus value, appropriated during the 20 weeks. If he had never made a profit, by forcing his workers to produce surplus value, he would be destitute. As it is he is rich. His capital is composed entirely of surplus labour performed by people who have worked for him during those weeks.

This is the logic of the system. Capital is past labour which has been appropriated by an exploiting class. Workers exchange their labour power against their own past labour. Because capitalists have appropriated workers' past labour, they are able to control their future work. Capitalists are able to exercise authority and control in the labour process because the machines and money capital are in their hands. These are obtained with previous profits. Within capitalism, workers' own past activity confronts them as a hostile and alien power, as capital.

As capital grows, the system expands. Surplus value is exchanged against more variable capital. More people sell their labour power and thereby put themselves under the authority and control of capitalists in the labour process. The social relations of capitalism spread.

These two closely related processes - the use of surplus value as additional capital and the spread of capitalist social relations - lie at the heart of accumulation. And accumulation is the normal way in which the system reproduces itself. Capitalism survives by growing.

3. Proudhonism and Capitalism

Diagram 3 (below) summarises social relations in four possible commodity producing societies. The first is the pure model of simple commodity production. Here there are no unequal or coercive social relations whatsoever. The second is an impure form of simple commodity production in which merchant capital predominates in the sphere of exchange. This brings the model one step nearer to the historical reality of artisanal production. Unequal and coercive relations exist in circulation. The application of proudhonist reforms to this type of society could in principle transform it into the first type. In other words, reforms could be sufficient to eliminate inequality and coercion

Diagram 3

Economic system	Social relations in production	Social relations in circulation
Simple commodity production	Freedom & equality	Freedom & equality
Simple commodity production with merchant capital	Freedom & equality	Inequality & coercion
Capitalism with merchant capital	Inequality & coercion	Inequality & coercion
Capitalism	Inequality & coercion	Freedom & equality

and thereby create an equitable society.

The third type is a capitalist system in which merchant capital again predominates in exchange. The successful application of proudhonist reforms would transform this system into the fourth type, a pure form of capitalism. While there are no unequal or coercive relations in circulation here, there are within production. Exploitation takes place at this level. The application of bourgeois-socialist reforms to capitalism would not produce an equitable society.

Such reforms would reduce the frictions to the operation of the law of value produced by trade monopolies but, if the value workers received in exchange for their labour power remained unchanged, would be of no help to the working class. They would simply alter the allocation of the surplus product between capitalists. Merchant capitalists would be driven out of business, allowing industrial capitalists to appropriate correspondingly higher profits because they could now buy materials more cheaply and sell products at higher prices.

Proudhon did not understand this. His political perspective

- which makes some sense in relation to artisanal production - is, as regards capitalism, fundamentally misconceived.

Marx's demonstration that capitalism necessarily involves inequality and coercion - central to the critique of proudhonism - also has contemporary political relevance. While the most influential variety of reformism today rests on rather different errors (part two), a significant residue of bourgeois-socialist thinking nevertheless exists within the labour movement.

Many people believe that the problem is not the existence of capitalism as such but rather that of particular types of capital. Scapegoats change. Sometimes, financial institutions and speculators are singled out; sometimes big, monopoly capital. Of course, certain sections of capital do at times act in particularly unscrupulous ways and make disproportionally large profits. But - as with the example of merchant capital above - if the value of labour power remains unchanged, this affects only the distribution of surplus value between different sections of capital. To regard a particular group of capitalists as the *fundamental* problem is to fall prey to the proudhonist illusion that a few central reforms - nationalisation of the banks or effective anti-monopoly legislation for example - could transform capitalism into an equitable system.

Secondly, it is widely believed that the fundamental reason why capitalism is unequal and hierarchical is that people become capitalists (or workers) as a result of a privileged social background (or lack of it). Locating this as the crucial objection to the system has proudhonist implications. It suggests that the right reforms could create an equitable, capitalist society - that a fully meritocratic capitalism would be synonymous with socialism.

Since the logic of the process of reproduction is that capital consists of previously produced surplus value, the way in which the money required to set up as a capitalist is initially come by is irrelevant to an evaluation of the system *as a system*. To think otherwise is to confuse the conditions which give birth to a mode of production - or to new units within it - with those of its self-renewal.

If the way capitalism had developed historically was that

certain frugal artisans had saved enough money to set up as capitalists, for example, then it could be argued that the conditions which gave birth to capitalism were perfectly equitable. In the extreme, it could be that all artisans had equal opportunities. Some chose to work shorter hours than others and to spend all their money on day to day living, while others chose to work long hours, consume very little and thereby save sufficient money to set up as small capitalists.

Similarly, new capitals which are constantly coming into being may begin life in a non-exploitative way. In some circumstances, individuals can still become capitalists by working hard and spending little. They save enough to become an artisan by buying into a small shop or a pub, say. After a time, as the business expands, they begin to employ people.

In practice, of course, the initial sums of money are not usually acquired in this way. Historically, money capital was mainly amassed by the operation of merchant capitalist monopolies or by straightforward plunder or fraud. Today, few capitalist enterprises are set up by people who have worked themselves up from the shop floor by their own efforts.

But this is not crucial. Even if every capitalist enterprise had its origins in an individual's hard work, this would not justify capitalism as a system. Because, once capitalism gets going, it is inherently and necessarily exploitative. However the original money was acquired, all capital is, after a point, previously appropriated surplus value.

The way in which an individual capitalist, or indeed the system as a whole, came into being is only relevant to moral judgements about individuals. It is *irrelevant* to an evaluation of the system as such. An extreme example may clarify this. Suppose that someone had just become a capitalist the day before socialism is established. He might argue that, unlike other capitalists, he should be compensated for the loss of his factory. While others' capital consists of previously produced surplus, his is made up of his life's savings. He has had no chance to exploit anybody. This would be the most he could legitimately argue. He could not reasonably claim that he should be permitted to remain a capitalist since this would necessarily involve exploitation.

Workers' co-operatives provide a final example of contemporary proudhonism. Many people see these as a solution to the exploitation inherent in capitalism. Such a perspective is essentially an attempt to adapt the ideal of simple commodity production to the current level of development of the productive forces, which rules out individual rather than group ownership of means of production by workers (see chapter 5).

It fails to take account of the compulsion exerted by the system to produce and accumulate the maximum possible surplus value. In order to survive, workers' co-operatives in competition with capitalist firms are forced to exploit their members as effectively as their capitalist counterparts exploit their workers. Even an economy composed entirely of workers' co-operatives would generate the same pressure so long as the law of value reigned supreme.

To conclude, it is impossible to devise reforms to eradicate inequality and coercion within the labour process and thereby create an equitable capitalist society. So long as the system is composed of competing units of capital, the exercise of authority and control within the factory is required to compel workers to produce surplus value. Without surplus value there is no profit and without profit no production.

This is not fundamentally a matter of the psychological make-up, social origin or even existence of individual capitalists. The system prevents those in control of units of capital - whether individual tycoons, shareholders and their appointed managers or co-operatives composed of the workforce - from acting otherwise by driving any who attempt to do so into the bankruptcy courts. Cigar-toting millionaires are in this sense an optional extra.

4. Living with Commodities

Historical materialism holds that the way economic activity is organised is crucial in determining the form of other social institutions and activities. Commodity production is no exception to this general rule.

The social relations of circulation are in principle the same under all forms of commodity production, although in practice they have only developed fully under capitalism. They are relations of freedom and equality in the market place. This way of organising the distribution of goods and services has far reaching effects, permeating almost all facets of society and giving them a form peculiar to the second great phase of human history.

The first section of this chapter traces ways in which relations of exchange influence people's perceptions of economic activity. Section two deals with their effects on other aspects of society. To return to the famous metaphor, it looks at base and superstructure in the present stage of historical development. The final section examines how the freedom and equality of circulation under capitalism act to conceal exploitation.

1. Commodity Fetishism

In commodity-producing societies, economic relations between people involve the exchange of objects. People meet on the market to buy or to sell. They exchange money for commodities or commodities for money. Commodities and money are interposed between people. Everything has its price and money enters into all economic relations. This is the basis for what Marx calls *commodity fetishism*.

Commodity fetishism is a difficult theory to grasp. This is partly because the term fetishism is rarely used in its original sense today. The dictionary definition of a fetish is an 'inanimate object worshipped by primitive peoples for its supposed inherent magical powers'. It has usually been created by the so-called primitive peoples. Today, however, fetishism has become associated almost exclusively with sex.

But commodity fetishism is difficult to understand for a more basic reason. We live in a world in which it exists. We are under its sway. It influences our perceptions and hinders thinking in ways other than those dictated by it.

There are two sides to commodity fetishism. Marx calls the first *mystification*. This describes the effect of commodity production on people's perceptions of its workings. People are mystified about the economic activities in which they participate. They do not comprehend them fully.

The other side to commodity fetishism is *domination*. People are dominated by inanimate objects which stand between, or *mediate*, their social relations. Marx put it as follows: 'their own social action takes the form of the action of objects, which rule the producers instead of being ruled by them'. People are dominated by money and commodities. Just like the primitive peoples of the dictionary, they are dominated by objects and processes they themselves have created.

Domination and mystification are closely linked. If you do not understand a process in which you participate, it is liable to dictate your response to it. You cannot control what you do not understand. It will dominate you. But domination and mystification are not synonymous and should initially be examined separately.

People are dominated by money and commodities because they are confined to responding to events. They act in the context of a situation which controls them. The events to which they react are changes in the prices of inanimate objects. They go to market with commodities - products in the case of artisans and capitalists, labour power in the case of workers - and sell them for the highest price possible. They then spend the money, buying the goods they need at the lowest possible price. People shop around the market for the cheapest loaf, or buy potatoes instead if these are cheaper.

People act to maximise both their income and the goods obtained with it. If prices change, they switch what they buy, what they make and who they work for. Behaving in response to the market is the only way in which individuals can act to protect their economic well being. Nobody controls that market. Everyone is dominated by the daily price list, over which nobody has control.

Commodity production relies on and develops a high degree of individual rationality. This is essential to the operation of the system. Without it, the law of value would not be able to work to allocate labour between industries in workable proportions.

But people acting entirely rationally as individuals may produce effects which nobody desires. Take the vexed question of public transport as against private cars. Today private transport is clearly inefficient, costly and polluting. In short, it is irrational. People wait for buses that never arrive because of traffic jams caused by hundreds of cars with one person in each. It crosses their minds that if the drivers went by bus, there would be pressure for a better service. Buses could move faster and everyone would benefit. But despite the overall irrationality of private transport, it may nevertheless be rational for each individual at the bus stop to buy a car. One person's virtuous decision not to buy one will not make public transport more efficient, and people can only act individually. No one has control over the market. It dominates everyone.

Commodity production involves *impersonal domination*. People are dominated by inanimate objects they have produced and by the market on which these are bought and sold.

Impersonal domination did not occur in the first great phase of human history. Under natural economy, domination was of a personal kind. People were dominated by specific individuals, not market forces; slaves throughout their lives by their master, serfs by their lord. Workers under capitalism are, of course, dominated in the labour process by their employer, but they are not forced to remain under the control of any particular one. They can acquire another by changing jobs. Although they cannot escape the tyranny of capital, they can elude that of an individual capitalist.

It may appear paradoxical to argue that people are domina- ted by commodities and also mystified by them. If domination is real, people are not imagining it. They react to changes in the market because it is in their interests to do so. Where is the mystification in that?

It derives from two features of commodity production. Firstly, the fact that the system evolved in a spontaneous manner. Serfs did not sit down one day, decide to abolish feudalism and institute artisanal production. No conscious decision was made. Secondly, the fact that commodity production is not consciously directed. It works on the basis of the decisions of individuals acting in their own interests. The law of value, not a ministry of planning, is the ultimate authority.

The features of the system affect people's perceptions of it. It seems always to have existed and destined to remain forever, rather like the solar system. Marx has an apt description for mistaking historically specific social processes which are con- stantly developing for permanent and immutable facts of life. He calls it believing them to be a *second nature*. This is one aspect of mystification.

Another is the way in which processes which result from the social relations of commodity production are seen as being physical properties of objects which mediate these relations. Marx writes of 'the fetishism peculiar to bourgeois political economy, the fetishism which metamorphoses the social, econo- mic character impressed on things in the process of social production into a natural character stemming from the material nature of these things'. He gives a number of examples. One concerns interest-bearing capital. In a mystified view of the workings of capitalism: 'it becomes a property of money to generate value and yield interest, much as it is an attribute of pear trees to bear pears'.

Of course, money-lending yields interest in certain societies, including capitalism. The profits that bankers make are not figments of the imagination. But the ability to earn interest is not a physical property of money, however natural the process seems.

Money yields interest because of the way production is organised in societies which practise money lending.

The attitudes towards money which commodity fetishism fosters show themselves in everyday language. It is commonly said that money buys baked beans, bombs or whatever, rather than that people buy these things with it. People are advised to make their money work; that is, to yield interest. They say that money talks, though few people have heard a £1 note speak.

The effects of commodity fetishism - of the impersonal domination of commodities, money and the market on which they are exchanged and of the mystified way in which economic activity is seen - are sometimes summed up by Marx in his later writings by the term *alienation*.

Both aspects of commodity fetishism are important politically. Because people mistake historically specific social phenomena for natural, permanent and unalterable properties of physical objects, they believe it possible only to adapt to them. To contemplate altering them seems outrageous; as futile or frightening as proposing changes to the solar system.

Marx calls ideas which are the product of a particular way of organising production and which mislead people about the real nature of the historical process *ideological*. The mistaken belief that commodity production is eternal is an important ideological basis for reformism. It is one reason why people adopt a reformist perspective. They cannot see any other option.

But a recognition that commodity production shrouds itself in mystification does not in itself free people from domination. Realising that your life is dominated by the impersonal forces of the market no more stops it being so dominated than a slave's understanding that he is someone else's property stops him being a slave. The only way to abolish domination, personal or impersonal, is to destroy the social relations which produce it and to construct a society which does not require it.

2. Commodity Production and the Superstructure

The spontaneous origin and unplanned nature of commodity exchange lead people to mistake social phenomena for the physical properties of objects. This is an important aspect of the ideology - the system of ideas - produced by commodity production.

This tendency to *naturalise* social phenomena is not restricted to the way in which people think about economic activity. It lies, for example, behind attempts to explain all observed differences between people in purely biological terms, whether in sexual habits or in so-called intelligence quotients.

Features of the domination involved in commodity fetishism also affect both people's ideas about themselves and the world around them and the ways in which they relate to each other. For the system to function, people must act as *individuals*. They must pursue their own economic interests by buying as cheaply as possible, selling at the highest price possible and switching jobs if the return is higher elsewhere, for the law of value to work.

One effect of this is that individuality is developed to a high degree in other areas of life. Because specialisation through the division of labour is a feature of economic activity, it is regarded as natural and healthy for people to concentrate on developing specific aspects of themselves. Some people read a great deal to develop their ideas. Others take to sport and develop their bodies. Some spend all their spare time playing darts or watching movies. It is regarded as normal to have individual interests and tastes. People are encouraged to develop their talents to find themselves a niche in the division of labour.

Most people live in isolated, self-contained units. Each house has its own cooking and washing facilities. Many people own personal means of transport. Individual privacy is regarded as an important aspect of freedom. It is thought rude in some circles to talk to people before being formally introduced.

The importance of particular individuals is often over-stressed. History books, for example, often give more weight to the abilities of individuals than to the social conditions which formed them and in which they operated. Marx makes this point when comparing his book *The Eighteenth Brumaire of Louis Bonaparte* with Victor Hugo's account of the same event, *Napoleon the Little*.

With him the event itself appears like a bolt from the blue. He sees in it only a single individual's act of violence. He does not notice that he makes this individual great instead of little by ascribing to him a personal power of initiative which would be without precedent in world history ... I show how, on the contrary, the *class struggle* in France created circumstances and conditions which allowed a mediocre and grotesque individual to play the hero's role.[1]

Another feature of the domination of the market, reflected in almost every aspect of contemporary life, is that people's relationships with each other are *competitive*. Whenever you meet someone on the market you are trying either to sell them something, in which case you want to charge as much as possible and they want to pay as little as possible, or to buy, with roles reversed. The typical sound of the market place is the babble of haggling.

The division of labour in commodity production involves interdependence between producers. None can live on the goods they alone produce. Everyone is compelled to rely on others. But this interdependence takes the form of intense competition.

This reflects itself in the superstructure. Education involves exams and grading. Sport is tremendously competitive; winning, rather than playing well, is often the object of participating. Prizes are awarded for creative activities such as painting and flower arranging. Success in competitions with others is the primary way in which people perceive themselves as worthwhile. This is often spoken of as the rat race.

The way of behaving which the individual and competitive nature of relationships produces is perhaps best described as *bourgeois individualism*. This is the common theme running through all institutions and activities in capitalist society. The components of the system are isolated individuals in competition with each other.

Under commodity production, people conceive their needs and aspirations on an individual basis. They need to be successful, famous or powerful to feel satisfied. The symbol of achievement is the acquisition of commodities. Advertising suggests that you could become more dynamic or sexually attractive if you owned such and such; to fulfil yourself as a person you are urged to consume. Individuals compete in terms of ownership and fashion, keeping up with the Joneses or Mick Jaggers of this world.

Another way to approach the relationship between base and superstructure is to examine ways in which non-economic areas of society exhibit a similar structure to that of exchange. Take the law.

The legal system in most capitalist societies is based on two fundamental principles: rights of property and of contract. The basic premise underlying the structure is that of individual private ownership. The legal world consists of individuals who own things.

This framework is stretched to fit legal entities like firms, which are treated as if they were people. A firm owns assets in law, in much the same way as a person owns clothes or a radio. The firm's right to keep, or to make a contract to sell, its property is more or less identical to a person's rights over their possessions.

Some of the 'things' over which legal entities - whether people or firms - have property rights are not inanimate material objects at all. They may be ideas, which can become somebody's property by the laws of copyright or of patent, or they may be people. Custody cases, for example, are essentially about which member of a separated couple will 'own' the children.

The legal world, then, is a world of commodities. It sanctifies and regulates the principles of the market. Everything from Westminster Abbey to Woolworth's is somebody's property and can only change hands by means of a freely agreed contract to buy and sell.

The political institutions which are thought of as normal - or at least presented as the ideal for which to strive - in capitalist society also mirror the activities of the market place. Parliamentary democracy is a reflection of commodity exchange. With elections on the basis of universal suffrage there exists a system of individual freedom and equality at the level of choosing, or (ex)-changing, a government. People vote in an individual, isolated fashion. The sum of their votes determines the composition of the government, just as the sum total of individual decisions about what to produce and buy determines the allocation of social labour. The freedom and equality of universal suffrage is real, as is the freedom and equality of commodity exchange. Both involve individual rather than collective decisions and actions - governments are chosen by secret ballots, not by collective public discussion and decision making.

As in commodity exchange, the freedom, equality and control apply only to the choosing, or (ex)changing, process. Workers have no control within the labour process under capitalism; neither do they have any control in the actual process of government. Once a government is elected, all authority resides in its hands. There is no democratic involvement in the execution of state power.

It is not only the public institutions of capitalism, such as parliament and the law, which correspond to the patterns of commodity exchange. Even the areas of life thought of as private and personal are structured by the principles of the market.

There are ways in which sexual relations quite literally take a commodity form. Prostitution is the sale of sexual acts. Pornography is big business. But it is not only the fringes of sexual activity that reflect commodity exchange.

Sexual relationships predominantly take a form which Engels described as *individual sex love*. They are based on a free contractual arrangement between two people. Often, a legal contract is signed during a marriage ceremony. After the contract is made, the couple generally live in an individual, isolated unit, bringing up children in a nuclear family. There is freedom of choice of sexual partner, as there is a freedom of choice on the market. Sexual acts, like commodity exchanges, usually involve only two people. This is the normal, respectable form of sexual relations under capitalism.

Thus almost all aspects of everyday life assume a particular form under capitalism; one corresponding to the underlying economic relations. Contemporary political institutions, legal systems and popular hopes and fears are products of a particular stage of historical development, just as are capitalist relations of production. This section has stressed this point rather than arguing the merits or otherwise of particular institutions or activities.

The most important political implication is that almost all facets of daily life are open to change. Socialism is about conscious, collective control not only of production but also of all other ways in which people relate to each other. Sexual relations, for example, need not always take the form of bourgeois marriage, aptly described by Engels as 'that state of leaden misery known as domestic bliss'.

3. How Exploitation is Concealed

Commodity fetishism and the other aspects of the super-structure discussed in the first two sections of this chapter are all effects of the social relations of commodity exchange. In principle, they are common to all forms of commodity production. Because they develop along with commodity production, however, they attain a more complete form in capitalist societies than in those involving artisanal production.

But there is an important difference between the social relations of capitalism and those of the model of simple commodity production. Capitalism involves exploitation, whereas simple commodity production does not. There is therefore a level of mystification about social relations under capitalism which is absent from artisanal production. As well as the fetishism which treats historically specific relations between people as eternal relations between objects, there is the commonly held belief that capitalist production does not necessarily involve unequal and coercive relations between people.

Where does this mystification originate? How is exploitation concealed within capitalism?

One feature of capitalism which acts to hide exploitation is the *wage form*. Workers acquire means of subsistence by being paid wages which they spend on commodities. Part of the way in which the wage form mystifies is that it extends the mystifications of commodity fetishism to labour power. Since labour power is bought and sold like any other commodity under capitalism, it is not exempt from the general confusions that exist about commodity production. To work for an employer who pays a wage seems as natural as it is, say, for money to bear interest.

But there is a more insidious way in which the wage form hides exploitation. Wages are normally paid after the work has been performed, at the end of the week rather than the beginning. While commodities are normally paid for when they change hands, workers are paid for their labour power only after it has been consumed in the production process. This may not seem important. The only real economic effect is that the worker gives the capitalist a week's interest-free credit. But the delay in payment induces confusion as to what precisely the capitalist is buying from the worker.

Because payment is made after the work has been done, it seems as though it is the labour performed, rather than the capacity for work, that is exchanged for a wage. The capitalist appears to buy labour rather than labour power. Wages, so people believe, tend to reflect the value produced by their work. They do not. They reflect only the value of labour power, the work involved in producing the capacity to work.

Misunderstanding about the nature of wages arises in part because services, sold as commodities, tend to fetch a price which reflects their value, the work put in. Under simple commodity production, a window cleaner, for example, would tend to receive the same for an hour spent cleaning windows as would a tailor for an hour spent sewing trousers. Similarly, a capitalist firm of window cleaners tends to receive the same rate of profit as a capitalist firm of tailors. The operation of the law of value ensures this in both cases (chapters 2 and 3).

Capitalist production is, for the capitalist, a means of producing a profit. He has no other reason for undertaking production. Employing workers would be futile if it did not yield a profit. To ensure this profit, capitalists must force workers to produce surplus value. If workers had to be paid the equivalent of the value they produced in capitalists' employment, no production would take place.

The illusion that wages represent the entire value produced by the worker is nevertheless strong. One of the central planks of reformism is the idea that a 'just wage' is possible within capitalism - 'A Fair Day's Work for a Fair Day's Pay'.

Under feudalism, the existence of exploitation is generally plain. The lords clearly get the benefit of the time serfs spend working on the lords' lands. The serfs' work on their own behalf to reproduce their labour power, and that performed on the lords' lands and producing a surplus are generally separated both in time and space. The two types of work are done on different days, in different places.[2]

Under slavery, necessary and surplus labour are not separated in this way. This gives rise to the illusion that all slave labour is surplus labour. After all, the slave master owns both the slave and the product. He pays no wages. But slaves must be kept alive if they are to continue working. Their owner must provide them with means of subsistence. Thus some slave labour is necessary labour, required to produce the food, clothing and shelter the slaves consume.

Under capitalism, surplus and necessary labour are not separated in time and space. Workers spend all their working time in the same factory. No one blows a whistle half-way through the day to announce that all work put in from then on is surplus labour. Unlike slaves, workers are paid a wage. The illusion is the reverse of that created by slavery: it seems as if workers are paid the equivalent of the full value they produce.

The wage form explains how the division between necessary and surplus labour is concealed. It explains how the *quantitative* side of exploitation is hidden. It does not explain how the actual *process* of exploitation - of capitalists compelling workers to perform surplus labour - is kept from view. Nor does it explain how the unequal and coercive relations within the labour process, which enable exploitation to take place, are hidden.

The wage form presents things in a mystifying way. It makes them appear to be other than they are. It is rather like viewing something through a telescope which, unknown to the viewer, distorts the picture.

As for the social relations of the labour process within capitalism, they are not presented in a distorted way. They are simply not presented at all. It is as if, this time, the telescope has a special filter which eliminates some features entirely. Because these are not perceived, it is easy to assume that they do not exist. Watching black and white TV, it is easy to forget that its tones represent colour. How is the capitalist labour process blocked out of the picture?

The answer is fairly straightforward because the process is a crude one. Bourgeois ideology - the way of looking at the world produced by the capitalist mode of production - relates only to the level of exchange. It simply does not take account of the way in which production, the most basic of human activities, is carried out. Both legal systems and notions of morality within capitalism generally ignore the coercive social relations of the labour process.

The law, for example, makes no distinction between the ownership of consumer goods and of means of labour. They are indeed equivalent at the level of exchange. The buying and selling of both involve free and equal social relations; the prices of both tend to reflect their values and so on. The law simply codifies this and institutes sanctions against people who violate the principles of exchange, by theft, for example. It takes no account of the different ways in which the commodities are used; consumer goods individually, means of production within a labour process which violates all bourgeois principles of freedom and equality.

Similarly, a capitalist or artisan agreeing to deliver a commodity in three weeks' time has the same legal status as an individual worker agreeing to work for a particular capitalist for a specified period. The law simply enforces the freedom and equality of voluntary agreement. It takes no account of the fact that the labour contract involves the worker in a situation which violates those same principles of freedom and equality which the law is supposedly protecting.[3]

The tendency of the capitalist mode of production to produce a superstructure based on the principles of exchange has other politically important effects. It means that capitalism is able to produce a far more liberal superstructure than those other class societies. This allows real gains to be won by the exploited classes. Universal suffrage, the right to free expression and so on are real advances for the working class. This liberalisation of the super-structure is possible because, under capitalism, unlike other exploitative modes of production, real freedom and equality exist in circulation.

This liberalisation of the superstructure is, of course, only a tendency. There are others countering it. Universal suffrage and the like have seldom been granted by the bourgeoisie without a fight. Constant vigilance is required to protect them. The nature of the counter tendencies and their strength in different historical periods are discussed below (part two). But whilst capitalism does not always generate a liberal superstructure, it does at times allow and even tend to produce one. It is unique as a class society in this respect. The gains which this allows must not be underrated.

It is nevertheless important to see the freedom and equality of commodity exchange and their superstructural effects in context. They are part of a system of production which is hierarchical and coercive. The freedom and equality of the market place are the means of imposing and maintaining the unfreedom and inequality of the labour process. It is therefore sometimes necessary for workers to forfeit some of that freedom and equality to make gains in the struggle against the capitalist class.

Many working-class victories have involved a restriction on individual freedom of exchange in the interests of workers as a whole. The formation of trade unions is an attempt to establish a monopoly position in the market for labour power in order to increase wages. The right to a closed shop is the right to prevent individual workers from making free contracts with an employer. Picketing is a weapon to enforce these restrictions on individual freedom.

Whether specific 'freedoms' should be supported depends on who benefits from them. 'Freedom' is not universally noble and good. To treat it as such is to fall into the trap of fetishism: seeing a historically specific social institution as a natural and eternal ideal. Take freedoms of speech and organisation. These always have a context. To discuss them outside of one is about as sensible as saying that a breadknife is a useful tool without taking account of whether it is in the hands of a friend making sandwiches or those of a homicidal maniac. The securing of such freedoms by fascist parties, for example, constitutes a major set-back for the working class.

This concludes part one, which has examined some important characteristics of commodity-producing societies. It has traced out the fundamental social relations of capitalism and the ways in which they are mediated by commodities and money. It has been concerned with structural features of the system and with their effects on other social institutions and activities.

The analysis has had a central political purpose. It was designed to provide both an explanation of the basis for bourgeois socialism - the type of reformism predominant in Marx's day - and a criticism of it. It located the origin of proudhonism in the overlap between artisanal production and capitalism and in a confusion between simple commodity production and capitalism, resulting from the misleading appearances of the latter. The critique focused on a demonstration that inequality and coercion are essential to capitalism.

Part two examines the development of capitalism over time. It is structured around the second, dynamic proposition of historical materialism - the idea that ways of organising production are at first historically progressive but, after a point, become a barrier to further development of the productive forces.

Again, the analysis has a central political purpose. It seeks to provide an explanation for both the continued existence of reformism and the changes that it has undergone, along with a critique of social democracy - the school of reformist thought which has been most influential throughout the twentieth century.

Part Two

Capitalism and the productive forces: the critique of social democracy

5. Early Capitalism

This chapter is concerned with the earlier phases of capitalism's existence. The first section looks at the ways in which the rise of capitalism was historically progressive. Section two draws out some political implications of the analysis.

1. Capitalism's Progressive Role

The picture most people have of early capitalism is one of child labour, dark satanic mills and other horrors of the industrial revolution. What was progressive about all that?

Historical progressiveness is the development of greater control by people over the world in which they live. There are two aspects to this. One is the extent to which people are able to transform nature to satisfy their wants. The other is the extent to which they can relate to each other in ways which further the development of their human capacities. In the categories of historical materialism, the first of these areas relates to the development of the productive forces and the second to the social relations within a society.

While both aspects of people's control over their environment are very important, for Marx, the level of development of the productive forces is more basic. This is because his theory of history holds that the productive forces are at some point hindered in their development by the social relations under which production is organised. The resulting tension creates the conditions for social revolutions, great leaps forward in history.

To assess the progressiveness or otherwise of a society at any stage of its development, it is vital to view that society in historical context. It is clearly absurd to gauge a society against a blueprint for an ideal world in which people have full control over nature and their own lives and to award it marks out of 10. There will be ways in which a society examined in its historical context represents an advance over its predecessor and others in which it creates possibilities for a successor to take the process further. Early capitalism was progressive in this double sense: looking both forward and back.

The image most of us have of the middle ages has been shaped by Hollywood. It is one of knights in shining armour and damsels in distress. Lately, chivalry has begun to give way to debauchery, though this has more to do with a relaxation of censorship than with a new-found quest for historical accuracy. Reality was less colourful than the versions depicted by either Errol Flynn or Pasolini.

Feudalism was the most advanced stage in the first great phase of human history, the period of natural economy. No really major advance in the productive forces had been achieved since the neolithic revolution: most people needed to expend all available effort on growing food, gathering fuel and other activities narrowly concerned with keeping themselves and their children alive. Production was therefore still largely agricultural.

The central social relation was that between serfs and feudal lords. Serfs were granted small strips of land on which to grow food and access to common ground on which to graze animals and to collect fuel in return for working on the lord's land for so many days a year. Because they had control over the land - an essential element of production in an agricultural society - lords were able both to force serfs to perform surplus labour and to appropriate the products of this labour. They were thus an exploiting class.

The principle of granting land and protection in return for labour services was not confined to the relation between lords and serfs. It operated at all levels of feudal society. A lord did not own the land on which his serfs worked. He was granted it by a higher lord in return for labour services. The higher lord was, in turn, granted his lands by someone higher up the scale. And so on up the hierarchy. At the top of the pyramid sat the monarchs and the pope.

But a lord's relationship with his serfs and that with his overlord differed in one important respect. Serfs worked for their lord in order to be able to work on their own lands. A lord, on the other hand, did not personally go to work for the next lord up the scale. Instead of keeping all his serfs hard at work performing surplus labour for himself, he passed some surplus labour on to his superior lord in the form of people to act as soldiers or retainers. The relation between lords and serfs concerned the *extraction* of surplus labour, whereas that between lords concerned the *distribution* of that surplus between members of an exploiting class.

Power and wealth in feudal society were based on land ownership. Control of the land brought with it command over labour services. Serfs, the people who did the work, were a mere adjunct to the land. If a piece of land changed hands, the serfs who worked it had a new master.

Capitalism was a major advance on feudalism in two senses. First, it cut the umbilical cord tying people to the land. It developed the productive forces sufficiently to enable a small proportion of the population to produce enough food for everyone. By releasing huge numbers of people from agricultural work, it made possible the production of all manner of previously undreamt-of goods.

Secondly, the development of capitalism radically undermined relations of personal dependency, replacing dependence on individual slaveowners and feudal landlords by impersonal dependence on the market. Despite the limitations of bourgeois individualism, the development of free and equal exchange, parliamentary democracy, equality before the law, individual economic rationality and the other developments described above (chapter 4) were major advances in people's ability to control their own lives.

There is no need to dwell on these points. Looking back over capitalism's shoulder, its development clearly represented an advance on feudalism. But the other side of its progressive role is less obvious. In what sense is capitalism a necessary bridge on the road to socialism?

As the section on the reproduction of capitalism (see chapter 3) showed, competition between capitalists forces them to extract surplus value from their workers and to accumulate this as additional capital. The pressure of the law of value compels capitalists to reduce their costs as much as possible by keeping wages low, expanding the scale of production and introducing more efficient techniques. Any capitalist who fails to do so will be driven out of business. Capitalists are just as subject to the impersonal domination of the market as are other buyers and sellers of commodities. They are under constant pressure to expand and to improve techniques of production. To survive, they must strive constantly to develop the productive forces.

Not all economic systems exert this kind of pressure. By and large it was not present before commodity production. For example, there was little incentive for a feudal lord to develop the productive forces. He would be more likely to use any extra surplus to maintain more soldiers and to dig a deeper moat to protect his station in life.

Under socialism there will not be any *economic* pressure to develop the productive forces. Decisions about how long to work, how much to consume now and how much to invest will be made collectively and democratically. They will be conscious *political* decisions, not, as under capitalism, necessities imposed on each individual by the operation of market forces. This does not mean that no development of the productive forces will take place in a socialist society. People may well collectively decide to forego some goods and services for a period in order to create a better world in the future. It means rather that decisions to develop the productive forces will be made with due consideration for the human costs involved.

This is important in understanding the historically progressive role played by early capitalism. Competition forced each capitalist to develop the productive capacity of his workforce as rapidly and effectively as possible. It forced him to act *without* consideration for the human costs involved. These costs were appalling, but the potential gains they created for the future of humanity were enormous.

Capitalism produced the greatest possible development of the productive forces for a period and thereby brought humanity's control over nature to a level at which the construction of a democratic socialist society is feasible. Attempts to build such a society before that development of the productive forces had taken place would have been doomed to failure. Democratic, collective control over production and investment at a very low level of development of the productive forces could only have strangled further development. It would be quite unrealistic to expect people with a very low standard of living to decide to work hard and to consume little in order to develop productive potential for the future. Capitalism only succeeded in getting them to do so by denying them any choice in the matter.

It is important to look at the ways in which capitalism developed the productive forces in some detail, for two reasons. First, it provides a basis for understanding - as far as is possible in advance - the possibilities for, and limitations on, socialism that history has bequeathed. Society can no more shake off its past than human beings can shake off their formative years. Both previous history and an individual's childhood can be transcended to some extent but in order to do this - to develop society or an individual as far as possible given historical circumstances - it is vital to understand the legacy of that history. To believe that the historical process which provided the building blocks from which socialism has to be constructed can be ignored and that, with enough good intentions, anything is possible, is to retreat into utopianism.

Secondly, it is important to examine ways in which capitalism developed the productive forces to understand how socialism can be brought about. It is not enough to say that the development which has been achieved under capitalism makes socialism possible in principle. Capitalism actually has to be overthrown and socialism built. It is essential to understand how the development of capitalism itself lays the basis for this, otherwise being a socialist would be about as sensible as being in favour of living on Pluto.

One legacy of the development of the productive forces under capitalism, which relates to the possibilities for and limitations on socialism, is a worldwide division of labour. Within a relatively short time after its initial development in England, capitalism had brought almost the entire world under its sway. It spread outwards like a prairie fire, destroying or permanently scarring and distorting everything in its path. Non-capitalist societies were either wrecked or subordinated to the needs of capital.

The motor force behind this was competition. The relentless pressure of the law of value, which forces each capital to strive to appropriate as much surplus value as possible if it is to survive, knows no geographical limit. Capital spread across the world with an insatiable appetite for cheap materials and markets in which goods could initially be sold at a high price because competition was ineffective. Just as more efficient capitalists drove out the less so, capitalism as a whole drove out less efficient modes of production.

As capital moved out from the centres where it developed, the state followed. It provided an armed force to subdue the native population and to protect its own national capital from foreign rivals. As well as acting as bodyguard, it provided certain basic facilities for capital. It organised the building of roads, railways, ports and so on to assist in exploitation. When one nation state gained control of an area for its own capital, it often consolidated its position by exercising formal political control. This was the process of colonisation.

One important implication of this aspect of the development of the productive forces is that socialism must be constructed on the basis of a worldwide division of labour. Specialisation provides enormous benefits in terms of a larger amount and wider range of use values with which human beings can satisfy their wants. As a result of capitalist development, workers in one town today transform materials from a dozen countries into goods to be sold all over the world. To try and return to any kind of national self-sufficiency in this day and age is like attempting to return to artisanal production in the early days of capitalism.

In fact, such attempts closely resemble the utopians' plans for model communities. In a world which has been thoroughly internationalised by well over a century of further capitalist development, a single national state today is the equivalent of a village in the 1840s. Attempts to concentrate on building socialism in one country must inevitably lead to a reactionary position, just as the utopians' attempt to build the New Jerusalem in one village did. The class struggle is now an international one. The Vietnamese liberation forces, for example, were not fighting the state power of their own bourgeoisie - which was more or less non-existent - but that of the French and US bourgeoisies in particular. For those whose priority is the construction of socialism in one country, the international class struggle becomes - just as did the national one for the utopians - at best a distraction from, and at worst an obstacle to, the task at hand.

A second aspect of the development of the productive forces, which relates both to the nature of socialism and to the manner in which it can be brought about, is capitalism's development of the most important productive force of all, the producers themselves. There are a number of sides to this process. One is the development of workers' needs and capacities.

It may seem strange to argue that the creation of needs is a progressive feature of capitalism. In recent years many radicals have pointed to the creation of 'artificial' needs as one of the system's worst features. They have argued that the thirst for profits leads capital to multiply the number of commodities available beyond any sensible limits and to use high pressure advertising to persuade people to buy them.

But the creation of needs and aspirations was a highly progressive feature of *early* capitalism. Feudal serfs had few desires beyond basic food, clothing and shelter. They seldom heard about events outside their village, let alone set foot beyond it. And even this, by contemporary standards, extremely limited horizon was not viewed in terms of rational self-interest. Things were the way they were because God planned them so. The tenacious hold today in some circles of irrational arguments against people exercising individual control over their lives, by contraception for example, shows clearly the impossibility of catapulting people with the outlook of feudal serfs into the second half of the twentieth century. Marx once put this point very strongly: one of the great merits of capitalism was, he said, that it did away with 'the idiocy of rural life'. The mental distance between that 'idiocy' and a taste for Clint Eastwood movies and holidays in Majorca is enormous.

It will not be easy to build a society in which people collectively, democratically and rationally decide on social priorities on a world scale. But it is now possible. It would not have been had capitalism not developed people's needs, aspirations and capacities.

There is a second aspect of the development of the proletariat, which relates to the overthrow of capitalism rather than to the operation of a socialist society. It concerns the way in which capital develops a class which is powerful enough to oust the bourgeoisie. The accumulation of capital is the reproduction of the system on an expanded scale, more capital and more workers. Thus, as accumulation takes place, the proletariat tends to grow numerically and so become stronger.

The accumulation of surplus value also tends to increase the size of each unit of capital. As a firm invests its profits, it grows. Marx calls this process the *concentration of capital*. This tendency is reinforced by another. Firms which fall behind in the competitive struggle experience losses and go bankrupt. Often, they are taken over by more successful rivals. Thus more efficient capitals can grow by means of the accretion of less efficient ones. Marx calls this the *centralisation of capital*. Capital therefore develops a proletariat which tends not only to grow in overall size but also to be concentrated in increasingly larger units of production. In this way, the working class is welded into a powerful social force.

The final aspect of workers' development to consider is the way in which capitalism develops a propertyless class with an interest in the abolition of private ownership of means of production and the creation of a classless society. Every exploited class has, by definition, an interest in abolishing the present system of production. It stands to gain from putting an end to exploitation because it suffers from it. But not all exploited classes have an interest in the abolition of private property. In a system of artisanal production dominated by merchant capital, for example, individual producers own means of production. They have an interest in doing away with merchant capital, but not in abolishing private ownership of means of production. They could be expected to fight to retain individual control over their means of livelihood. To understand the specific nature of the exploited class created by capital, it is necessary to look at the changes in the process of transforming nature brought about by accumulation.

So far, discussion of the development of the productive forces has been restricted to an explanation of ways in which competition forces capitalists continually to revolutionise techniques of production. This demonstrated how the social relations of circulation, based on free and equal commodity exchange, force capital to bring about changes in production techniques. But changes in the social relations of production itself are also crucial to the development of the proletariat as a class with a unique historical role.

Marx distinguishes three stages in the development of relations within the capitalist factory. At first, factories differed little from expanded artisanal workshops. Craftsmen carried out their trade much as before, but gathered together under the same roof.

There were some changes, of course. There was, for instance, a saving of means of production. If a particular tool was only used occasionally, a factory employing 30 people might only require three or four, whereas independent artisans would have needed one in each workshop. Organisation and the exercise of authority also became separated out as specific, independent tasks. Although master artisans had been in a position of authority over apprentices and had played a larger role in organising the work process than the latter, this task took up relatively little of their time and was not considered to be a specific job. Once a large number of people came to work under the same roof, things changed. To use an analogy of Marx's, while one or two instrumentalists can play together without outside direction, an orchestra requires a conductor. The question is: who gets the job? In the factories the capitalists did because they owned the means of production.

Finally, some processes were now done collectively. If the factory owner required a heavy object moving, for example, he might order everyone to stop whatever they were doing and lend a hand. Such tasks required more people than were found together in an artisanal workshop. Marx took his name for this phase of the capitalist labour process from this feature. He called it *co-operation*.

Despite these differences, normal relations between workers, and those between each worker and his tools, differed very little from those of artisanal production. The intrinsic nature of the work process remained much the same. Craftsmen retained their skills and with them the possibility of becoming independent artisans again if only they could acquire means of production. Capital had yet to devise a distinctive labour process of its own.

Marx calls the second stage, which dominated capitalist production from the mid-sixteenth century to the last third of the eighteenth, *manufacture*. The crucial difference between co-operation and manufacture is that the latter involves a division of labour within a craft. The various stages of a trade were broken down and parcelled out between different workers. Thus, instead of, say, 40 watchmakers working side by side as under co-operation, there would, under manufacture, be 3 hand-assemblers 4 spring-attachers, 2 cog-wheel fixers and so on. Watches would still be made in the factory, but no individual would produce a complete one.

This development increased the output of a given number of workers in a given time. It meant that workers became skilled at the particular part of the overall process in which they specialised. With practice at it, they became faster than they could be at a wide range of skills. Specialised workers also developed better tools for particular jobs. They no longer had to switch from one task to another, and therefore could save the time involved in putting down one set of tools and picking up another.

As well as these fairly obvious gains in efficiency, the development of manufacture brought other important but more subtle changes in the labour process. A certain regularity in the intensity of labour began to be imposed within the work process itself. If people worked side by side making complete shirts, they could to some extent choose the pace at which they worked. But once one person stitched on the collar, another the right arm and a third the left, they had to establish a similar rhythm if the overall process were to proceed smoothly.

The organisational role played by capitalists also grew in importance. They had to decide how to break down old crafts and distribute workers between jobs. Was it better to have one or five people sewing fronts, back, collar and sleeves together? How many cutters were needed in relation to machinists? As well as conducting the orchestra, capitalists now had to write the score.

Workers gradually lost any chance at all of escaping from the factory to become artisans. The problem was no longer that they simply lacked means of production. They were also losing the range of skills required to produce a complete commodity.

Marx calls the third stage of capital development that of *modern industry*. This final major change was ushered in at the end of the eighteenth century by the industrial revolution. The crucial feature of this stage is that production is organised around systems of machines. The machines are set to work in concert with each other at controlled speeds. Workers have to adapt their operations to the rhythm and pace of the machinery. They become, in Marx's words, 'mere appendages of machines'.

The examples of modern industry which most easily spring to mind are relatively recently innovations. Consider a conveyor-belt system. Workers stand next to a moving surface onto which a machine lowers bottles, say, every 30 seconds. They have to check that the bottles have caps on, set upright any which topple over and reload the machine with caps from time to time. This basic pattern of work, radically different to craft production, was inaugurated not by the invention of conveyor belts and assembly tracks but by the industrial revolution. For example, tending a power-operated loom in the nineteenth century was an essentially similar operation.

With the development of modern industry, capital acquired the way of organising the work process best suited to its needs. The dependency on old craft skills was broken, so that cheap unskilled labour could be used for many jobs. The machinery, controlled by capital rather than by the workers, determined the pace of work. Stretching the analogy a little, capital now not only conducted the orchestra and wrote the score but had also succeeded in replacing musicians by machine minders who had only to press buttons to perform a symphony.

These changes in the process of transforming nature had important implications for the future development of society. First, they ruled out a return to artisanal production and thus rendered proudhonist programmes for establishing a pure form of simple commodity production totally utopian. No one can set themselves up in business with a two-foot length of a car assembly track and the ability to fit left-hand doors.

Secondly, production within each capitalist enterprise became more and more directly social. All commodity production is indirectly social. It is based on a division of labour in which nobody is self-sufficient. Everyone depends on other people's work to provide them with the range of use values they require. Even simple commodity production would be social in this sense, though each artisan might work in isolation from others.

But capitalism develops social production in a more direct way. As accumulation takes place, those capitalists who survive the competitive process employ larger numbers of workers operating increasingly sophisticated machinery. They have to decide how best to combine workers and machine systems. The market forces them to do this, since if they did not, they would be unable to compete and be driven out of business. But the market does not do the job for them. It is conscious control, not the law of value, which decides on the most efficient use of capital within a factory. Wise capitalists set up their own little internal planning ministries.

The development of planning within a capitalist enterprise is in clear contrast to the anarchic nature of the economy as a whole. Once the existence of such planning is acknowledged, regulation by the market ceases to seem natural and eternal. Planning becomes a part of everyday reality. It becomes easier to conceive of its extension. The conscious direction and control of economic life which will take place under socialism begins to develop, albeit in a hierarchical and coercive form, in the womb of the capitalist firm.

The accumulation, concentration and centralisation of capital has created a class powerful enough to overthrow the existing order. The development in workers of needs, aspirations and the potential capacities to fulfil them has created a class capable of running a socialist society. The development of modern industry has created a class whose future can lie only in socialism. Capitalism has brought about a development of the productive forces which rules out any return to artisanal production. With modern techniques, production must take place on a large scale and be consciously directed. Collective and democratic control is the only way to achieve this without exploitation.

Early capitalism was therefore progressive in many ways. It enabled people to control their environment to a far greater extent than was possible previously and, most importantly, it fulfilled some essential historical tasks. On the world scale there is no way in which it could have been bypassed. Those who fought against its development and tried to set up alternative forms of society were misguided.

2. Reforms and the Early Workers' Movement

New recruits to the factories resisted wage labour from the earliest days of capitalism. The degree of resistance varied from area to area and struggles took a variety of forms. But they had one feature in common: a tendency to view the struggle from the perspective of a desire to return to the old order. Ruined artisans yearned for the good old days of independence; landless peasants for a mythical, liberal feudalism. Both groups tried to reverse the historical process, to run the film backwards.

The various strands of early socialist thinking reflected these reactions. They refined general resistance and nostalgia for an idealised past into more or less systematic social philosophies on the basis of which they tried to build political movements. Marx's criticisms of this perspective were outlined earlier (see chapter 1).

This response was inevitable. Capitalism had yet to develop sufficiently for factory workers to see themselves as members of a new class with particular interests of its own. The proletariat was small and weak. It had little power to assert itself as a distinct entity. In these circumstances, it was bound to associate itself with the groups and classes from which it had emerged.

But capitalism developed and the situation changed. As accumulation took place, more people were recruited into the proletariat. With the development of manufacture and then, most importantly, modern industry, old skills became obsolete. People came to see themselves primarily as factory workers, rather than as craftsmen of one kind or another. As this happened, trade unions developed. Thus the proletariat began to take shape as a powerful class with distinct economic interests of its own and organisations to fight for them.

On the political level, workers were initially educated and mobilised by the bourgeoisie for its own ends. As the capitalist class grew in economic importance, it demanded corresponding political power. It fought to wrest control of the state away from the representatives of feudal society. Initially, the bourgeoisie allied with the monarchy against other pillars of the old order, the barons and the church. Later, the capitalist class turned to its own creation, the proletariat, for support in a fight against its former ally.

The inherent logic of the accumulation process and the bourgeoisie's need for support against the old order leads it to create a social and political force which is ultimately antagonistic to it. In so doing it undermines itself from within. It is in the unfolding of this process, rather than in movements to set up model communities or to press through proudhonist reforms, that marxists see the real possibilities for socialism.

But the process takes time. During its early development, capitalism was a vital and progressive force. The bourgeoisie was a revolutionary class, destroying the old order and laying the necessary groundwork for socialism. The latter was not on the immediate agenda. The proletariat was insufficiently developed to overthrow capitalism and to construct a society capable of serving its interests. For a considerable period, 'the whole historical movement' was, in Marx's words, 'concentrated in the hands of the bourgeoisie'.

How were marxists to operate during this period? What programmes and policies were they to put forward? Which groups and organisations were they to support and which to oppose?

Marx and Engels laid down general guidelines in *The Communist Manifesto*. Where no significant workers' movement yet existed, communists were to support bourgeois groups and parties in their fight against the representatives of feudalism. This would hasten the destruction of the old order and promote the development of capitalism and of the proletariat.

At the same time, they were to help create independent workers' parties and, once these existed, to work to strengthen them. Priorities were to achieve unity among the workers, to build up their experience of political activity and to educate them in a scientific understanding of the historical process. A crucial aspect of this latter task was criticism of other socialists. These priorities were to take precedence over the winning of individual battles.

This perspective implied that when workers' parties were in their early stages, it was often correct to urge them into alliance with parties representing the bourgeoisie. Such alliances would serve three main purposes. They would give proletarian parties valuable political experience. They would speed up the development of capitalism and hence the overall historical process. Finally, they would give workers a say in the way old institutions were destroyed and in the form of new ones built to replace them. Thus the proletariat could press for the development of those forms most beneficial to itself. In the fight to replace absolute monarchy by parliamentary government, for example, it could fight for the widest franchise.

In the early stages of capitalist development, then, communists were not to form their own political parties, separate from others representing workers. They were to strive for united proletarian parties. Within these, they were to distinguish themselves from other groups in two ways. First they were to press for policies which furthered the interests of the class as a whole, rather than those of any group within it. This implied placing the development of the class internationally before that of any national section and giving longer term effects of policies and actions priority over possible short-term gains. Secondly, and of course relatedly, communists were to explain the nature of the historical process to other workers, so as to dispel illusions as to the possibility of short-cuts to socialism.

This sober perspective, based on the assessment that the fulfilment of certain essential historical tasks by capitalism was a prerequisite for socialist revolution, clearly implied a sustained policy of fighting for reforms. Communists were to assist the bourgeoisie in reforming away remaining feudal fetters on the development of the productive forces and to press for these reforms to be as radical as possible. Given this, what distinguished Marx's perspectives and programme from those of reformists?

Marx's approach differed from Proudhon's in the important respects outlined earlier. Basically, the proudhonists failed to appreciate crucial differences between simple commodity production and capitalism and hence believed that reforms designed to remove impediments to free and equal exchange would be sufficient to transform capitalism into a free and equal society. Marx had no such illusions.

With the development of capitalism and decline of artisanal production, however, the workers' movement inevitably became less influenced by proudhonist conceptions and more concerned with reforms relevant to the world in which it lived. It increasingly fought for reforms which would improve its lot under capitalism, rather than supposedly laying the basis for a society of free and equal independent producers. Thus the day to day policies of Marx's supporters came to resemble more closely those of groups concerned solely with winning reforms.

But a crucial difference between the two approaches remained.

While, for many, reforms were purely an end in themselves, for Marx they were primarily a part of the means to a more important end. The fight for them was one element in an overall strategy, based on perspectives derived from an understanding of capitalism as a stage in the historical process.

Marx's analysis indicated that both the possibility of and the need for advancing beyond reforms would increase as the system developed. As capitalism began to outlive its historical usefulness as a world system and become a barrier to further progress, the struggle for reforms within it would develop into one for its revolutionary overthrow.

This would not be a mechanically pre-determined event, like a solar eclipse. It would rather be a process whose tempo was influenced by the behaviour of participants. Workers would both build up their own strength and weaken that of the system by struggling to overthrow capitalism. But a successful outcome was nevertheless ultimately dependent on the world capitalist system becoming an obstacle to further development of the productive forces.

Disagreement over this perspective constitutes the fundamental difference between marxists and reformists. The origins of modern reformism lie in a rejection of Marx's position by prominent members of the international labour movement at the turn of the century and in the organisational split to which this led. This is discussed in the next chapter.

6. Rotten Capitalism

This chapter is largely concerned with a debate which took place around the turn of the century about the limits to capitalism's progressive role. The first section examines the relationship between accumulation and crises. This provides a basis for understanding and assessing section two, a discussion of different interpretations of the stage of capitalist development reached at the time of the debate. The third section discusses some political conclusions drawn by participants. An examination of this debate is essential to an understanding of modern reformism, the central features of which first emerged at this time.

1. Crises and Over-Accumulation

Two aspects of accumulation have been discussed so far: the reproduction of the system (chapter 3) and the development of the productive forces (chapter 5). A third aspect, considered here, is the difficulties capitalism experiences in the course of its self-expansion.

Marx laid great stress on disruptions in accumulation. He called them *crises* and wrote that:

> Crises ... by their periodical return put on its trial, each time more threateningly, the existence of entire bourgeois society ... The productive forces at the disposal of society no longer tend to further the development of the conditions of bourgeois property; on the contrary, they have become too powerful for these conditions, by which they are fettered, and so soon as they overcome these fetters they bring disorder into the whole of bourgeois society.[1]

In other words, crises are an important aspect of the way capitalist social relations become, after a point, a barrier to further development of human beings' ability to transform nature.

Crises characteristically bring unemployment and idle machinery. All the elements of production - materials, means of labour and people to work them - exist side by side. Yet capitalists do not bring together machines and workers because it is not profitable to do so. There could be no clearer indication that the way production is organised can restrict utilisation of the productive forces, let alone further development. Crises are thus harbingers of social revolution.

Despite the importance Marx attached to crises, he nowhere laid out a systematic analysis of their causes. He intended to do so but, because crises are among the most complex of economic events, he felt a discussion of them should follow an analysis of all major features and developmental tendencies of the system. As it turned out, he died before completing the task.

Marxists have, however, since developed a number of theories based on Marx's fragmentary remarks and, more importantly, his general theoretical framework. This section discusses the more important of these.

Reproduction is never entirely trouble-free in any society. The simplest economic system imaginable would run into problems. One in which individuals grew their own food and were entirely self-sufficient, for example, would experience unexpected bad harvests, droughts and so on.

More complex societies face further difficulties. Any system involving a division of labour experiences problems in allocating labour between the production of different goods. No mechanism is capable of always achieving a perfect balance. In a socialist society, for example, mistakes in drawing up and implementing economic plans will inevitably occur because future events are necessarily uncertain.

In commodity-producing societies, this problem is intensified because production is anarchic. The division of labour is not planned. Instead, it is regulated by the law of value - an imperfect mechanism at the best of times.

Suppose that, as a result of an unexpected change in society's preferences, too many cars have been produced. Capitalists in the motor industry are either left with unsaleable cars or compelled to reduce prices. Their profits suffer. This overproduction of cars is, of course, accompanied by a corresponding underproduction of other goods, which society now desires relatively more of. Thus capitalists in other industries have experienced unexpectedly high demand and made greater than average profits.

If the law of value worked to reallocate labour between industries in precisely the proportions society now desired, exactly the required number of capitalists would move from car production into these under-supplied industries. This may happen. But it is far from certain to.

Capitalists in the motor industry may assume the change in preferences to be temporary. Rather than investing elsewhere, they may simply cut back production while waiting for demand to pick up. If this happens, difficulties will develop throughout the economy.

Car producers will reduce their orders for steel, rubber, machine tools and so forth. Capitalists making materials and machines for the motor industry will experience reduced demand for their products. Their profits will fall. Since car workers who have been sacked are no longer receiving wages, demand for consumer goods will fall. Capitalists producing means of subsistence will thus face similar problems. Profits will decline here too.

Once underway, this process continues under its own steam, gathering momentum as it does so. Capitalists supplying the motor industry buy fewer machines and materials and lay off workers. The same happens in means of subsistence industries. Soon the whole economy is affected. The fall in sales and production spreads outwards and grows like ripples on a pond.

The result is a *slump*. Unemployment grows. Machines lie idle. The productive forces are held back.

The above is an example of a crisis arising from an imbalance between the supply of and demand for different goods. The initial problem was a lack of proportion between production and demand in particular industries. Disruptions arising in this way are usually called *disproportionality crises*.

Some aspects of the example have a general relevance for understanding crises. One is the fact that the descent into slump is propelled by *realisation difficulties*.

The downward spiral of production is triggered off by a section of capitalists not spending its profits. Other sections - suppliers of goods to this industry - then experience realisation problems as markets for their products are reduced. It is the conditions for realising surplus value, rather than for producing it, which deteriorate; first for this group of capitalists then for others. The *immediate* mechanism for a spiralling downward into slump is always the spread of realisation difficulties.

This leads to the second general point illustrated by the disproportionality example: the fact that the onset of realisation problems must itself be explained. In the example, realisation difficulties are sparked off by a group of capitalists deciding not to invest because its profits have suffered as a result of an imbalance between the supply of and demand for a particular good.

Finally, it is of general relevance that the realisation difficulties begin with a failure to spend on the part of capitalists. Such difficulties could in principle originate either with capitalists failing to spend all or a part of their profits or with workers failing to spend all or a part of their wages. But in practice the latter is highly unlikely. Workers use their incomes to maintain themselves and their dependents. While individual workers save, others borrow and thus spend more than they earn. For the working class as a whole, saving and borrowing are usually more or less equal. A *sharp* fall in the proportion of workers' incomes spent, capable of triggering off a slump, is extremely unlikely.

Not so with capitalists. By and large, they do not spend profits on personal consumption. They invest them to make further profits. There is thus a plausible situation in which they will not spend their incomes: one in which it does not appear profitable to do so.

While accepting that disproportionality can lead to crises,

many marxists have also sought other causes. They have argued that disproportionality is unsatisfactory as a sole explanation of crises because it lacks the force of necessity. While imbalances between the supply of and demand for different goods are inevitable, because of the anarchy of capitalist production, they need not result in crises. The law of value may work to correct them relatively painlessly in the manner outlined previously (see chapters 2 and 3). For instance, in the example above, capitalists in industries experiencing increased demand may borrow unspent profits from the motor industry to expand their investment. The revolutionary case would be strengthened if a systematic tendency towards crises could be shown, over and above the likelihood of their following from 'accidental' imbalances.

Some attempts to demonstrate this emphasise a shortage of workers' demand for means of subsistence. This approach is usually called *underconsumptionalist*. The grain of truth in it is the fact that realisation difficulties almost invariably begin with a failure to spend on the part of capitalists. Thus the smaller the proportion of output consisting of means of subsistence the larger the proportion that must be realised by capital and hence, in one respect, the more unstable the edifice.

But it is fatuous to argue that the cause of crises is therefore the fact that workers' wages are insufficient to realise all output. If they were sufficient, there could be no profit and hence no production under capitalism. All attempts to construct a rigorous underconsumptionalist theory with the force of necessity have either involved a failure to appreciate that capitalists' expenditure can be sufficient to realise all surplus value or, in the case of versions which claim that workers' expenditure must grow less rapidly than the production of means of subsistence, required illegitimate assumptions to sustain the argument.

Another approach concentrates on the accumulation process. Recognising that competition compels capitalists to strive for the maximum rate of profit and of accumulation, it seeks a cause of crises in a tendency for the rate of accumulation to exceed that which the system can sustain and thereby to undermine the conditions for profitable production.

A demonstration that a fundamental tendency towards *over-accumulation* and resulting crises exists would constitute a powerful criticism of capitalism. It would show that there is a more fundamental problem than frictions in the working of the system. If accumulation tends after a point to produce problems for the future reproduction of the system then it is just that aspect of capitalist social relations which is central to the system's progressive role that turns, by its own inner logic, into a barrier to further development.

The most influential attempt to show this is based on a *tendency for the rate of profit to fall* which is held to result from a rise in the value of constant capital per worker. The argument can be expressed as follows.

Competition forces capitalists regularly to replace existing production techniques with more advanced ones involving more machinery per worker. Thus the tools used in artisanal workshops have, for example, been replaced over time by huge machine systems. Hence in the course of capitalist development, the value of constant capital (k) rises in proportion to that created by living labour ($v + s$).

Given this, the rate of profit $\left(\frac{s}{k+v}\right)$ must fall unless the rate of exploitation ($\frac{s}{v}$) rises sufficiently to offset the faster increase in k than in $s + v$.

But there is a limit to how long s can rise sufficiently to offset the effects of the relative increase in k. As v shrinks in relation to s, the possibilities for increasing the latter by further reducing the former diminish. At the extreme, when v becomes a negligible proportion of $v + s$, s cannot increase faster than $v + s$. With k growing more rapidly, the rate of profit must eventually fall.

This tendency for the rate of profit to decline will, it is argued, lead to uneven and sometimes sharp falls in the actual rate of profit. The fall is uneven because other developments such as changes in the rate of exploitation work to offset or to intensify the underlying tendency. Sharp falls in profitability trigger off realisation problems as capitalists are unwilling to invest in such circumstances.

Influential as this theory is, it is quite untenable as a theory of crisis. Two crucial weaknesses are discussed below. While the first is perhaps easier to grasp, the second is more devastating.

Even if the *physical quantity* of means of labour per worker tends to increase, it does not follow that the *value* rises. The value of constant capital depends on both physical quantity and time involved in production. The labour time embodied in tools and machines tends to decline over time as workers engaged in their production themselves become equipped with improved means of labour. This tendency, which works in the opposite direction to that of any increase in physical quantity, is just as fundamental an aspect of the development of the productive forces. Thus the value of a machine tool produced by labour utilising another such tool may equally well be greater or less than that of a set of files and saws, which the machine tool replaces, produced by workers equipped only with files and saws. No systematic tendency for k to rise in relation to $v + s$ exists.

Further - and this is the second criticism - no new production technique which capitalists decide to introduce ever yields a lower rate of profit than would have accumulation using the old technique. Thus the introduction of a new method of production can *never* in itself cause a fall in the rate of profit, regardless of whether or not it involves an increase in constant capital per employee. A simple example may indicate why this is so. (Formal proofs are cited in the guide to further reading).

Suppose a capitalist discovers a new technique of production. If it is more expensive than the old method he will have no incentive to introduce it. If it is cheaper, he will. In the latter case, his profits rise. Soon all capitalists in the industry adopt the new technique because it reduces costs. So long as output remains the same, the rate of profit in the industry rises above that in the economy as a whole. But other capitalists are attracted into the industry by the high profits. Output rises and price falls until the rate of profit is brought down to that in other industries.

If the commodity is a means of production, other capitalists' costs are reduced and the overall rate of profit rises. If the commodity is consumed by workers, means of subsistence become cheaper. If this enables capitalists to pay lower wages, profits rise. Otherwise workers' living standards improve as they can now buy more goods. The *real wage* - the amount workers can buy with their wage packets - rises. In no case do profits fall.

A general decline in profitability can only occur if a rise in real wages sufficient to offset any effect on the rate of profit of improved techniques takes place. An explanation of crises based on over-accumulation must therefore show how accumulation tends to bring about such a rise.

A crucial factor in over-accumulation is the peculiar status of labour power within capitalism. In circulation, labour power is a commodity like any other. It is bought and sold and its price is subject to changes in supply and demand. In production, however, labour power is not a commodity. It is not produced for exchange. The social relations in which conception, birth and child rearing take place are not those of a capitalist factory.

This frustrates the operation of the law of value. If the balance between the supply of and demand for labour power is disturbed, the system initially responds as normal. If demand declines, price falls. If demand rises, so does price. But the response ceases to be normal at this point. With any other commodity, a change in price would prompt one in supply. If price fell, production would become less profitable and capital leave the industry. If price rose, profitability would increase and capital enter. This does not happen with labour power because capital cannot flow into and out of its production.

Historically, the supply of labour power has often exceeded demand. This was especially so in the early days of capitalism. The dissolution of feudalism and artisanal production created a flow of potential new workers. The development of manufacture and modern industry increased the range of suitable labour power as skills became less necessary. Women and children were brought into the factories, often displacing men. Marx described the generation of unemployment in the course of capitalist development as the creation of an *industrial reserve army*.

But excess supply of labour power itself works to increase demand. As with any commodity, when supply is high in relation to demand, price tends to be low. Low wages imply high rates of profit and accumulation and hence a rapid growth in demand for workers.

Further, while the processes which work to create a reserve army are ever-present effects of accumulation, their quantitative importance tends to decline with the development of capitalism. Once production is predominantly capitalist, the inflow of ruined artisans and the like declines to a trickle. As more and more of the population become wage workers, sources of additional labour power dry up.

In developed capitalist societies, the fundamental tendency is therefore for accumulation to exhaust the industrial reserve army.

Whenever this happens, the rate of growth of the demand for labour power exceeds that of supply. If this were not so, full employment would never have been achieved since the reserve army would have been growing as fast as demand for workers. Thus the onset of full employment always indicates that the existing rate of accumulation cannot be sustained. Since competition compels capitalists to accumulate surplus value, a reduction in the rate of accumulation requires a corresponding one in the rate of profit. This can be brought about in a number of ways. The simplest is as follows.

As labour power becomes scarce, capitalists compete to buy sufficient quantities. The price is bid up. Wages rise. As this happens, capitalists withdraw from operation machinery which, because it is technologically backward or wearing out, can no longer be used profitably at the higher wage level. Eventually, sufficient workers are released from working with old machines to operate all newly-installed ones. Each time surplus value is accumulated, this process is repeated. Wages rise. Costs increase and surplus value is correspondingly reduced. Profits fall.

At some point, capitalists cease to invest in the face of declining profits. Realisation difficulties set in, bringing about a descent into slump.

To summarise, the motor force in a downward spiral into slump is the spread of realisation difficulties. This process is almost invariably triggered off by some capitalists deciding not to invest. Capitalists so decide when they are dissatisfied with the prospects for profitability. Such dissatisfaction may result from a temporary imbalance generated by the anarchy of production.

But a fundamental tendency towards a decline in overall profitability also exists. This flows from a tendency for the rate of accumulation to exceed that which the supply of labour power can sustain. This generates difficulties for the *production* of surplus value and hence dissatisfaction with the prospects for profitable investment.

2. Progress, Collapse or Decay?

The origins of modern reformism lie in a debate which took place in the international workers' movement during the very last years of the nineteenth century and the first two decades of the twentieth. This debate split the movement, first theoretically, then organisationally, into two opposed camps.

The debate was initiated by a series of articles written by Bernstein in the late 1890s and later expanded into a book. The central issue of disagreement was the interpretation and accuracy of the dynamic principle of historical materialism as applied to the transition from capitalism to socialism. In other words, the argument was concerned with Marx's ideas about historical change and their application to the construction of socialism.

Both the timing and form of the debate were influenced by preceding economic and political developments. It is therefore important to examine briefly the context in which it occurred. The major economic factors are discussed below, while the political ones are considered in the next section.

Capitalist development in the nineteenth century had been punctuated by recurrent crises and slumps. Because of the shortage of statistical information, economic historians are not fully agreed about the timing of these crises. Reasonable estimates might be 1825, 1847, 1857 and finally the 'great slump' of 1873. Accurate dating is actually relatively unimportant. There is general agreement that crises occurred at approximately ten year intervals until the latter part of the century, when they became less frequent but, most would argue, more severe.

There is some dispute about the duration of the great crisis which began in 1873. But it seems to have been generally accepted at the time that it was the last to occur in the nineteenth century. Certainly none of the participants in the debate questioned this.

Another feature of economic development in the last decades of the nineteenth century was an increase in the scale and power of larger units of capital. In part, this resulted from the normal processes of concentration and centralisation. But, in addition, a more novel development took place. In some industries, the major firms came together into associations which divided up the market between themselves, controlled the level of production, fixed prices and so on. The big firms were called *monopolies* and the associations they formed *cartels*. Again, all the participants in the debate agreed that these developments had taken place.

Bernstein accused the leaders of the Second International - the major international working-class organisation of the time - of believing that crises would become more and more severe, eventually reaching a point at which capitalism would no longer be capable of functioning. This 'final crisis' would usher in socialism. He called this view a theory of *breakdown* or of *collapse*.

Bernstein argued that such a position was incorrect. In his opinion, Marx had never envisaged a final breakdown of the system. He had suggested that crises would tend to become more severe but was mistaken. The experience of the period since 1873 had shown that accumulation was becoming more stable rather than less so.

The principal explanation for this relative stabilisation lay, Bernstein argued, in the development of cartels. By fixing prices, output levels, market shares and so on between themselves, the cartels were able to effect a degree of planning. Thus major disruptions to production and accumulation could be and were being avoided. Capitalism was developing the productive forces rapidly and would continue to do so for the foreseeable future.

Bernstein not only argued that contemporary marxists were mistaken about the point at which capitalist social relations had or would become a barrier to the development of the productive forces. He also insisted that for all practical purposes it was wrong even to consider the possibility, which, in his view, could only lie so far in the future that speculation about it should not be allowed to influence political strategy. This amounted to a rejection of a central tenet of historical materialism.

Marxists responded to Bernstein's criticism in two ways. One was to insist that capitalist production must collapse at a certain point and to attempt to demonstrate this theoretically. Thus began a long debate which has come to be called the *breakdown controversy*. This is not discussed here, largely because marxists today agree almost unanimously that there is no necessity for such a breakdown.[2]

The other response to Bernstein was to argue that capitalism had already reached the point at which it constituted a barrier to further development of the productive forces. This required an analysis of world capitalism in the phase of development it was then undergoing, paying particular attention to the significance of cartels. This approach proved the more fruitful for marxism.[3]

Important contributions were made by, amongst others, Bukharin, Hilferding and Kautsky. A full discussion would take a book in itself. This section concentrates on the most influential - Lenin's in *Imperialism, the Highest Stage of Capitalism*. The purpose is not to try to provide - or to suggest that Lenin provided - a fully adequate account of the phase of capitalist development then reached. It is rather to give an indication of ways in which leading marxists tried to utilise and develop Marx's theory in analysing a later stage of capitalism.

Lenin's *Imperialism* was written some twenty years after Bernstein's original articles and had the advantages of being able to draw both on work produced during the intervening period and on a knowledge of the actual course of economic and political development over the two decades, including the outbreak of the first world war.

The title of Lenin's pamphlet often gives a misleading impression to modern readers. Today, the term imperialism is usually used to describe unequal and oppressive relationships between advanced economies at the centre of the world capitalist system and those at the periphery, which are euphemistically described as 'underdeveloped' or even 'developing'. But as Lenin makes clear in the first sentence of his pamphlet, at the time of writing, the term was commonly applied to the characteristics of the era as a whole. It is in this wider sense that he uses the word. He describes the purpose of the work as the presentation of 'a composite picture of the world capitalist system in its international relationships at the beginning of the twentieth century'.

Lenin's analysis takes as its starting point two fundamental tendencies of capitalist development: the tendency towards the concentration and centralisation of capital and the tendency towards over-accumulation. He saw contemporary developments in capitalism as the results of the forms in which these tendencies revealed themselves and interacted.

By the turn of the century, he argued, the concentration and centralisation of capital had reached the point at which many industries were dominated by a few large firms. A parallel process had produced a situation in which the bulk of money and credit was under the control of a handful of powerful banks. Once the bulk of production within an industry was under the control of a few giant firms it was fairly easy for them to come to some agreement about the amount to produce, the price to charge and so on. Hence cartels.

This process was given a helping hand by the big banks. As more and more deposits and loans passed through their accounting systems, they became able to assess the strengths and weaknesses of their customers, monitoring both those making huge profits and those dangerously in the red. They had no particular favourite. If one firm drove another out of business, they were left with the debts. Banks had an interest in the restriction of cut-throat competition and the formation of cartels.

Their control over the purse strings allowed them to play an active role in the process. They could give credit on generous terms to those firms willing to participate in cartels and withhold finance from the unwilling - a powerful lever.

As industry came to depend more and more on the banks for

funds and the latter put an increasing amount of money into industry, the two developed a close relationship. Hilferding coined a term for this merging of banking and industrial capital which Lenin adopted. He called it *finance capital.*

The interconnected processes of concentration, centralisation, the formation of cartels and the development of finance capital were given a boost, Lenin argued, by the over-accumulation of capital. The great slump of 1873 and its aftermath brought a spate of bankruptcies. Many capitals were driven out of business or taken over by their erstwhile rivals. The lack of investment opportunities led to idle money capital being channelled into the banks, strengthening the latter.

Over-accumulation and centralisation led to the export of capital on a massive scale. Cartels moved abroad to gain control over sources of essential raw materials as a way of keeping other capital out of their lines of production, thus safeguarding for themselves control over these. Lack of investment opportunities at the centre led to the export of money capital. Banks in particular lent money overseas, often to foreign governments.

This intensified export of capital from the system's centre to its periphery led, by the beginning of the twentieth century, to a situation in which almost the entire globe had come under the sway of metropolitan capital. Markets and sources of materials were divided up between the big cartels. Markets for loans and financial securities were similarly parcelled out between the major banks.

This economic division was paralleled by a political one. Colonisation reached the point at which a handful of advanced capitalist countries had political control of almost the entire world. Like the cartels, the governments of these countries made, broke and remade alliances with each other, manoeuvring to maintain positions of power.

The division had grown up piecemeal over the course of time and did not reflect the relative economic strength of the major powers at the turn of the century. England, the earliest developer, controlled more of the world than its strength warranted. As the world was carved up, it became more difficult for late developers to gain influence commensurate with their economic strength on a world scale by acquiring new sources of materials, markets and colonies. Germany therefore colonised a disproportionately small area, a mere tenth of the size of British possessions, with only a twentieth of their population. Eventually the division was completed.

After this point, changes in the world balance of power necessarily involved a *re-division*. Since no major untapped markets existed, a cartel could only obtain additional ones by depriving a rival. Similarly, a state could only increase its colonial empire by reducing that of a rival state. Because the initial division of territories between the major capitalist powers had not been proportionate to their relative strengths, which were in any case constantly changing, pressures towards a redivision were inevitable.

For this reason, Lenin argued, agreements within and between the big cartels were necessarily temporary. When one cartel, or one firm within a cartel, grew more powerful it would demand an increased share of the market. Other cartels, or firms, would resist any redivision which reduced their share. When tensions became too great, agreement would give way to cut-throat competition.

The regulation of production, on which Bernstein put so much emphasis, would give way to greater anarchy and instability than existed in the days before cartels. There would be price-cutting, the withholding of raw materials, restrictions on international trade imposed by capitalist governments and all out economic warfare. Crises would become more severe.

Similar developments would occur on the political level. International agreements about colonial possessions would be violated by countries whose economic strength was not matched by the size of their empire. Thus economic warfare would be accompanied by military conflict. Capitalist states would fight for colonial markets with tanks as well as tariffs. Lenin saw the war of 1914-18 as the first example of this new type of inter-capitalist conflict.

Lenin's analysis of capitalism's development was thus

diametrically opposed to Bernstein's. The coming years would be ones of stagnation, crises and wars. Capitalism had turned the corner. It had become a barrier to the further development of the productive forces and was moribund - literally, at the point of death. The objective conditions were ripe for socialism.

Lenin's analysis is still the source of controversy. It certainly has weaknesses. Theoretically, it is less well developed than either Hilferding's or Bukharin's work, on which much of it is based. Lenin's theory of over-accumulation is obscure to say the least. His concentration on German development led to a considerable exaggeration as to the extent of the merger between banking and industrial capital.

But it also has strengths. It is perhaps the most comprehensive attempt since Marx to construct an overall account of one particular stage of capitalist development. Unlike Bernstein's picture, it is based on an analysis of fundamental tendencies of capitalist development in operation, even if in places a weak one. Its analysis of inter-capitalist struggles for the re-division of the world has become almost universally accepted within marxism.

Finally, it contains a brilliant prognosis as to developments in the first half of the twentieth century. This was a time of decline and decay. After the first world war, a brief boom was followed by the worst slump capitalism had yet experienced: industrial production fell by 13 per cent between 1920 and 1921. Only eight unstable years later this was dwarfed by the onset of the great depression of the 1930s. Industrial output fell by 35 per cent between 1929 and 1932 and unemployment in four major capitalist countries alone reached the colossal figure of 30 million people. Full employment came only with rearmament and six years of total war in which all major capitalist countries participated. Overall, little economic progress took place. The productive forces stagnated.

3. Revolution or Reform?

Certain of Bernstein's political positions are similar to those of earlier socialists which Marx criticised. The progressive role Bernstein attributed to co-operative stores is, for instance, reminiscent of utopian plans for model communities. Bernstein in fact explicitly links Proudhon with Marx as the joint precursors of his own position. Behind these specific points of overlap lie two more general and pervasive similarities.

One is a confusion between historically specific relationships between people and eternal and natural relationships between things; in other words, a tendency to fall prey to commodity fetishism. Like many of his socialist predecessors, Bernstein treated institutions specific to a certain stage of historical development as absolute, eternal ideals. He saw private property in this way. Thus he was horrified by the policy of expropriation without compensation, which he described as 'robbery dressed up in legal form' and 'wholly objectionable'.

A particularly important case of this general confusion is his analysis of bourgeois democracy. Rather than seeing this in context - as a form of government which had grown up in certain historical conditions on the basis of a particular mode of production and was subject to the limitations of that stage of development - he regarded it not only as an ultimate ideal but also as a panacea for all problems.

Thus he argued that whereas feudal institutions had been 'unbending', and had had to be overthrown by violence, those of 'modern society' were 'flexible' and did not therefore need to be destroyed, only developed further. While universal suffrage was admittedly only a part of the process of creating a socialist society, it was 'a part which in time must draw the other parts after it as the magnet attracts to itself the scattered portions of iron'.

This first general similarity between Bernstein and the early socialists is closely linked to the second, a belief that socialism could be achieved by gradual reform of the existing system. This belief, common to both Proudhon and Bernstein, is the defining characteristic of reformism.

Despite these similarities, however, Bernstein's ideas differed from Proudhon's in a number of crucial respects. Unlike Proudhon, Bernstein did not confuse capitalism with simple commodity production. The reforms he advocated were relevant to workers rather than to artisans.

Secondly, Bernstein did not see a clear dividing line between capitalism and socialism. In a sense, neither did Proudhon. He failed to recognise that capitalism necessarily involves unequal and coercive relationships and hence to understand that the construction of a free and equal society entails its abolition. But he did define socialism in terms of universal freedom and equality. There was, for Proudhon, a distinction to be made between the ultimate aim and the numerous partial reforms that were a means to it.

Bernstein, on the other hand, would emphatically have no truck with such aims. Among his aphorisms, the following express the position: 'Unable to believe in finalities at all, I cannot believe in a final aim of socialism.' And again: 'To me that which is generally called the ultimate aim of socialism is nothing, but the movement is everything.' Thus, while for Proudhon and Marx reforms were a means to an end, for Bernstein they were everything. There was no end. Socialism was nothing more than the reforms themselves and the movement that fought for them.

Bernstein's politics flowed logically from his analysis of capitalist development. As he saw it, capitalism would not only be able to develop the productive forces indefinitely but also come to experience less and less disruption in the process. This made possible the continual extension of democratic reforms. The liberal superstructure that early capitalism had tended to develop could, he believed, be refined without limit. This process was what Bernstein understood by the term socialism.

It is no coincidence that he was a member of the German Social Democratic Party (SPD). This organisation had been more successful in recruiting support than any other workers' party of its time. It gained half a million votes in 1877 and was promptly banned under the Anti-Socialist law of 1878. Despite this setback, its support grew until, shortly after the repeal of the law in 1890, it received one and three quarter million votes, over one quarter of those cast. It was regarded as a model party by the rest of the international workers movement.

Bernstein was proud of this achievement and wished to see it continue. He felt that the day to day struggle for reforms in which the SPD engaged was the key to its success. This was only hampered, in his view, by reference to the limits of the process and to the eventual need for the overthrow of the system. The SPD should give up such 'outworn phraseology' and 'make up its mind to appear what it is in reality: a democratic, socialist party of reform'.

The marxist response to Bernstein attempted to provide both a critique of his political strategy and an explanation of why it arose when and where it did. At the same time, it sought to develop an alternative approach.

As with economic analysis, marxist debates on political strategy of this period were amongst the most fruitful ever. It is impossible in the space available to give an adequate account, let alone an assessment, of the discussions. The rest of this section concentrates on three of the most influential ideas put forward. It seeks to give an indication of both the scope of issues confronted and the gulf separating the spectrum of marxist opinion from that of Bernstein and his supporters.

Luxemburg argued that it was now possible to go beyond the struggle for reforms in practice as well as propaganda. Capitalism had fulfilled its historical role. It had developed the productive forces sufficiently to make possible the construction of socialism. In the process, it had created a proletariat capable of overthrowing it. Revolution was now on the agenda.

Furthermore, the old approach had reached its limits. The main obstacles to accumulation met by capital in its early days were external, vestiges of natural economy. Capital broke them down by subordinating all facets of society to the rule of the market. The principles of free and equal commodity exchange became the new gospel to be applied to all areas of life.

But the main obstacles capital now encountered were internal to the system. They were its own creation, results of previous accumulation. Thus the problems were no longer those of establishing the rules of commodity exchange. They were rather the results of having played the game according to those rules.

The accumulation of capital had brought cartels, colonies

and crises. These developments had intensified rivalries between major capitalist states. To maintain or improve its position vis-à-vis competitors, the capitalist class in each country required an increasingly centralised state with a military apparatus capable of subduing and defending its own colonies and of filching others from its rivals.

The main class opponent had changed too. The feudal aristocracy had long since been beaten. Capital now had to fight its own offspring, the proletariat. The enemy was within and growing stronger on a diet of reforms.

Thus, Luxemburg argued, the bourgeoisie needed to abolish much of the individual freedom and equality introduced in the course of struggle against the aristocracy. The intensification of inter-capitalist competition and of the class struggle meant that the capitalist class could less and less afford legal and political systems based on the freedom and equality of exchange. It needed to extend the hierarchical and coercive relations of the labour process to other spheres of life. Over-accumulation and mono-poly thus brought reaction and violence in their wake. The basic tendency was now towards some form of totalitarian rule by the bourgeoisie.

Thus, while it was still correct to fight to win further reforms and to defend previous ones, there was very little future in this policy in and of itself. Many previous gains had become incompatible with the needs of capital and could only be defended by means of the revolutionary overthrow of the system.

Luxemburg's analysis applied essentially to advanced, metropolitan-capitalist countries; those with relatively developed bourgeois-democratic institutions and a powerful proletariat. But what of backward countries at the periphery of the system? Were they simply one stage behind? Must they experience a period of progressive capitalist development before becoming ripe for socialism?

Trotsky argued that this was neither necessary nor possible. The notion of progressive and non-progressive stages in the life of a mode of production was only applicable at a world level. The backwardness found at the periphery of the system was of a very different nature to that which had existed in Western Europe before the development of capitalism. It was the result of a particular pattern of capitalist development rather than of the absence of any such development.

Rather than evolving in the same way in each country, capitalism had followed a pattern of *combined and uneven development*. Advanced countries had integrated backward ones into the world capitalist system primarily as sources of materials and of agricultural products. The development of the periphery was thus inextricably bound up with that of metropolitan capital, but followed a distinct path: one determined primarily by the needs of the advanced countries.

This prevented the emergence in backward countries of a bourgeoisie sufficiently powerful to carry through the democratic reforms characteristic of early metropolitan-capitalist development. Thus the periphery would not experience this progressive process. But some of its effects were nevertheless present. In particular, the importation into certain sectors of the most up to date examples of modern industry - developed at the system's centre - created a very advanced, if small, proletariat.

The weakness of the bourgeoisie in the periphery not only prevented it from carrying out the historical tasks undertaken by its counterpart in the advanced countries but also made it possible for the proletariat to play a role quite out of proportion to its size. The possibility existed there, Trotsky argued, for many of the tasks elsewhere performed by the bourgeoisie to be combined with those of a socialist transformation into a single revolutionary process led by the working class. He called this audacious perspective one of *permanent revolution*.

Lenin sought to explain both the emergence of Bernstein's ideas and their influence within the workers' movement. Much of the explanation of their arising where and when they did could be found in the immediate economic and political context of Germany in the late 1890s. The importance of the relative economic stability of the preceding years, of the development of cartels and of the successes of the SPD has been indicated above.

But Lenin was writing some twenty years later, during the first world war. Relative stability had given way to the bloodiest inter-capitalist war in history. Privation, conscription and the suppression of trade-union rights were the order of the day, hardly progressive reforms. Yet Bernstein's ideas retained widespread support. This required some explanation.

According to historical materialism, political philosophies and parties are just as much products of particular societies as are legal systems and forms of the family. They develop on the basis of modes of production and reflect the interests of classes or groups within them. Thus bourgeois socialism, for example, reflected the interests of artisans. Lenin argued that Bernstein's ideas reflected the interests of, and drew their main support from, a relatively privileged section of the proletariat.

The export of capital and the carving up of the world market by cartels and capitalist states had created a situation in which, according to Lenin, capital at the centre appropriated surplus value from colonies as well as that produced by workers at home. To use his terminology, metropolitan capital appropriated *super profits*. A part of these were used to pay high wages to sections of workers at home to ensure their acquiescence in the system. Lenin called this *bribery*.

This stratum of workers - which Lenin, following a remark of Engels's, called the *labour aristocracy* - had an interest in maintaining the status quo. It reaped benefits from the worldwide system of exploitation. While in favour of reforms which would improve its position, this group would not support policies which might endanger the capitalist system as a whole, in which it had a stake.

This part of Lenin's analysis is the subject of considerable controversy. The evidence of historical research is on balance against it. But it does have the merit of explaining two aspects of Bernstein's politics which cannot be accounted for purely in terms of his analysis of capitalist development or of his fetishisation of bourgeois democracy. One is his opposition to certain basic, liberal reforms. He did not support demands for the right to work, for example, or for the automatic right to state benefits for the unemployed. He was also opposed to free provision of legal assistance. This is explicable if his policies represented only the interests of a relatively privileged and secure section of workers.

The other particularly reactionary aspect of his politics was his view that workers' parties should defend the interests of their national capitalist state. He defended this position by arguing that, once workers had the vote, they had a share in the common property of the nation. Thus he was against the abolition of standing armies and even in favour of the acquisition of colonies in certain circumstances.

Again, this can be explained in terms of the interests of a privileged section of workers. The privileges, vis-à-vis the rest of the working class, depended on capital appropriating super profits from the rest of the world. The relative strength of 'their own' bourgeoisie internationally was thus important to this group.

When the first world war broke out, the SPD acted on this last position of Bernstein's. As rivalries between major capitalist states exploded into armed conflict, SPD representatives in the German parliament voted finance for the war effort.

Lenin and the orthodox marxists argued that this was a violation of the fundamental principle that the interests of the working class as a whole had precedence over those of any section. By voting money for the war, the SPD was allying with the German bourgeoisie against both the bourgeoisie *and the workers* of other countries. In effect, it was taking the position that German workers had more interests in common with German capitalists than with French or English workers.

Lenin and his supporters broke from the Second International on this issue. When sufficient resources had been amassed, they set up the Third International to co-ordinate and direct the revolutionary wing of the workers' movement throughout the world. This differentiation in policies and in organisation required one in terminology. Previously, the workers' movement as a whole had been referred to, and had referred to itself, as *social-democratic*. Now the members of the Third International called themselves *communist* and the term social-democratic was reserved for the reformists.

The marxist analysis implied a view about the development of the class struggle in the period ahead. Capitalism's inability to develop the productive forces would lead to further stagnation, crises and wars. This would reduce profitability, undermine the conditions of existence of the labour aristocracy and force the bourgeoisie to adopt increasingly coercive forms of rule. The basis on which the Second International rested would crumble. The working class would become disillusioned with social democracy and be won over to the Third International. Thus the coming years would see both the revolutionary overthrow of capitalism and the construction of a worldwide socialist society.

This prognosis was generally confirmed by events over the next twenty years or so. These were indeed times of stagnation, conflict and decay. The bourgeoisie was forced to employ increasingly barbaric methods of rule. Fascism replaced more liberal forms of government in a number of countries. Large sections of the working class came to reject reformism and to embrace a revolutionary marxist position. As Otto Bauer, a leading member of the Second International who wholeheartedly supported Bernstein at the time of the split, said in 1936:

> The experience of Fascism destroys the illusion of reformist socialism that the working class can fill the forms of democracy with socialist content and develop the capitalist into a socialist order without a revolutionary jump.[4]

The one prediction not borne out was that of the revolutionary overthrow of capitalism. Despite the Russian revolution of October 1917 and major battles for state power in other countries, a worldwide socialist system was not established. For reasons which lie beyond the scope of this book, the Third International failed to lead workers to power. Capitalism survived.

7. Capitalism Since the War

This chapter brings the story up to date. The first section registers the considerable development of the productive forces that occurred during the 1950s and 1960s and examines its effects on social democracy. The second briefly analyses the crisis to which this period has given way. An appreciation of the main factors involved in this is essential to an understanding of its effects on reformism, which are assessed in the concluding section.

1. The Reprieve

The second world war left much of the capitalist world in chaos. Although the loss of life and destruction of means of labour were not very significant economically, the damage to capitalist social relations was enormous.

In the summer of 1945, disruption in the defeated powers was such that production was reduced to between one half (France) and one tenth (Japan) of pre-war levels. The old state machinery had collapsed in many countries. Governments had been brought down by a combination of foreign armies and internal resistance movements. Armed workers' organisations were in control of factories and mines, some of which they were operating under workers' management. These organisations and armies faced each other uneasily. Both were armed.

Workers in the armies on both sides had had enough of war and the bourgeoisie could not be sure of maintaining military discipline. Workers who had not fought on the battlefields had suffered considerable hardships. They had worked long hours.

There had been shortages and standards of living had been depressed. Industrial unrest flared up after a period of relative quiescence.

At the time, most observers thought the chances of a sustained period of capitalist expansion to be low. Their prognoses ranged from the pessimistic to the catastrophic. In fact, the period from the early 1950s to the late 1960s saw just such an expansion. These years, now referred to almost universally as the *long boom*, saw not only relative peace and prosperity but also a major development of the productive forces.

The reasons for both the initial re-stabilisation and subsequent long boom are the subject of dispute among marxists. Important though this question is, it is not discussed here. This section registers the extent of the boom and examines its effects on reformism.

The boom should not be underestimated. Between 1952 and 1968, world capitalist production doubled.[1] Thus one half of the use values produced annually in the world today result from development of the productive forces during those 16 post-war years. This is an impressive achievement. It is also historically unprecedented. There are no other periods on record during which growth was as rapid and sustained.

Moreover, the process seemed, while it lasted, remarkably trouble free. World capitalist output grew in every one of those 16 years. The proportion of the population in employment in the capitalist world as a whole never fell by more than one percentage point. The productive forces were highly utilised and developed rapidly. Capitalism appeared to be experiencing a second childhood.

The boom brought a reprieve for social democracy as well as for capitalism. This is hardly surprising. Reformism tends to flourish in periods when capitalism develops the productive forces. Such developments create circumstances in which reforms can be won. Economic growth makes wage increases, reductions in working hours and other economic reforms possible without endangering accumulation. The social stability that full employment and rising living standards tend to bring permits political reforms. The bourgeoisie has less need to move to totalitarian forms of rule in periods of stability and growth.

Reforms also appear sufficient to large sections of the labour movement at such times. They offer tangible gains without the threats of insecurity and violence which inevitably accompany a revolutionary perspective. Thus social-democratic ideas and their supporters in workers' parties were reinvigorated by the boom.

Post-war social-democratic philosophy was most coherently expressed, and to some degree moulded, by a book called *The Future of Socialism* written by Anthony Crosland in 1956. The title is a misnomer. What Crosland discusses in the book is the future of capitalism.

Crosland's position is partly a repetition and development of Bernstein's. There are a number of clear similarities. Thus Crosland shares Bernstein's belief in the importance of the co-operative movement and his tendency to fall into the trap of commodity fetishism. In Crosland's case, this last weakness is expressed in the view that alienation is a product of modern technology as such, rather than of the social relations within which it is utilised. Behind these obvious similarities lie two fundamental ones.

One is the belief that capitalism can develop the productive forces indefinitely without experiencing severe crises. Crosland bases this position, as did Bernstein, largely on the experience of the immediately preceding years. This is assumed to continue into the foreseeable future. But a fairy godmother is once again held to have brought about the change. While Bernstein saw cartels playing this role, Crosland casts the state in the part. He argues that governments now possess the knowledge and ability to prevent crises occurring. Here Crosland was uncritically following a shift in bourgeois academic opinion, which had become converted to a set of ideas known as *keynesianism.* [2]

Although keynesianism did not gain widespread acceptance until after world war two, the central ideas were developed during the 1930s slump. At the time, orthodox economists argued that the slump persisted because trade unions prevented wages from falling. This kept profits, and hence production and employment, low.

The keynesians objected that a cut in wages could only worsen the situation by further reducing expenditure. The solution, in their view, was for the government to initiate public works schemes such as road building. As workers employed on these spent their wages, markets would increase. This would prompt capitalists to invest and to re-employ workers.

The best formulation of the theory underlying these proposals is Michael Kalecki's. In the simplest version, all incomes consist of either wages or profits. The latter are sub-divided into those retained by firms and those distributed to shareholders. All wages are spent on consumer goods and all retained profits invested. Further investment is financed by borrowing. Distributed profits are saved. If distributed profits exceed borrowing, a deficiency of expenditure exists. The resulting shortage of markets leads to a slump. This tends to be self-perpetuating as profits and hence the incentive to invest are low.

The state can intervene at an early stage to prevent a slump setting in, or initiate a climb out of slump at any time, by itself undertaking expenditure equal to the difference between borrowing and saving.

It should be clear that the basic insight contained in the theory is the fact that capitalists must themselves realise all surplus value if reproduction is to proceed smoothly (see chapter 3). Kalecki expresses this general point in terms of a particular model. He divides capitalists into two groups: high-level management and major shareholders. The former make all investment decisions. If they decide to borrow less for investment than shareholders save, realisation difficulties result.

The practical conclusions drawn by the keynesians - that slumps can be avoided by the state making good any shortfall in expenditure - possessed obvious attractions for social democrats. They appeared to deliver a theoretical coup de grâce to marxist claims as to the inevitability of crises. Thus Crosland could argue that keynesian policies would allow a social-democratic government to ensure crisis-free development of the productive forces.

The other crucial similarity between Crosland and Bernstein is an almost absolute faith in parliamentary democracy. Like

Bernstein, Crosland regarded development towards this as both irreversible and sufficiently powerful to ensure the democratisation of all aspects of life and the adoption of socialist policies. Thus he derides the view that the British ruling class might in certain circumstances revert to undemocratic forms of rule as 'an echo from another world'.

Belief in crisis-free development of the productive forces for the foreseeable future and in the inevitable extension of bourgeois democracy to all spheres of life are the classic hallmarks of social democracy.

But Crosland's analysis and policies go beyond Bernstein's in a number of respects. Analytically, there are two main differences. One is Crosland's belief that further development of the productive forces is becoming increasingly irrelevant within advanced countries. 'The threshold of mass abundance' has been reached.

The second major difference is that, unlike Bernstein, Crosland did not regard the contemporary world as capitalist. He argued this by pointing out a number of differences between present-day society and that of the nineteenth century (some real, some spurious) and arguing that the marxist criterion defining capitalism - the class ownership of the means of production - is incorrect. The features of society which marxists claim result from this class ownership are, in his view, an inevitable product of large scale production, however organised.[3]

In fairness, it should be pointed out that many reformists with views similar to Crosland's would not agree with him on these last two points. They cannot be regarded as defining characteristics of post-war social democracy.

Crosland's political policies were an advance on Bernstein's in two important respects. Firstly, Crosland did not restrict his programme to reforms benefiting better-off workers. He was thus a more consistent reformist than was Bernstein.

Secondly, Crosland was less concerned with extending democratic institutions than was Bernstein and more concerned with policies for which social-democratic parties should fight within such institutions. This change in emphasis did not reflect less concern for democracy. It came about because the most important of those institutions - parliamentary democracy with universal adult suffrage - had finally been won in many advanced capitalist countries.[4]

The central thrust of Crosland's policy was the re-distribution of resources from rich to poor. Social-democratic parties were to campaign on this basis and, once in government, to use the state apparatus to implement such policies. The rich should be taxed more heavily than the poor and the money used to finance free state provision of certain services, such as education and health, and the payment of subsidies to the worse off in the form of social security, old age pensions and the like. In this way, a minimum standard of material welfare could be provided and both a reduction in inequality and an improvement in workers' living standards achieved.

Thus, while marxists see the fundamental inequality within capitalism as that between workers and capitalists within the labour process and believe that other inequalities derive from this, the post-war social democrats concentrated on inequality in living standards. While marxists see the development of the productive forces as the most important basis for improving living standards, and hold that capitalism has outlived the phase during which it was the most effective vehicle for such development, Crosland and his supporters assumed this to be unproblematic and concentrated on the distribution of goods and services. Finally, while marxists see the capitalist state as a product of the economic system, and one whose form tends to be democratic in some phases and totalitarian in others, the Croslandites regarded it as a universal tool for ensuring both economic stability and a redistribution of income.

The most effective critique of Crosland's ideas is an analysis of developments during the last decade. As the next section shows, such an analysis reveals how the developments of the boom years undermined the system in the very process of maintaining it. Capitalism's negative side has now come to the surface. As it becomes visibly less healthy daily, the strains imposed by 20 years of rapid expansion become more obvious.

2. The Current Crisis

Had this section been written five or six years ago, it would have been necessary to argue that a crisis existed. Today everyone knows that. The *Financial Times* and *The Economist* regularly carry articles which would until recently have been considered unjustifiably alarmist by many revolutionaries.

But, while the existence of a crisis is now generally recognised, its nature and causes are not. Governments and the media usually discuss each economic problem in isolation. They concentrate on one at a time and present that as *the* crisis. The last few years have seen, amongst others, 'the dollar crisis', 'the crisis of inflation', 'the oil crisis' and 'the crisis of sterling'.

This approach fulfils a function for capitalism. It suggests that the difficulties are unrelated and limited in extent. The political implication is that only minor modifications to the system are required. Small institutional adjustments, a little more co-operation from the trade unions or a few US marines in the Middle East would be sufficient, it is suggested, to restore stability. Since nothing fundamental to capitalism is at fault, nothing fundamental need be changed.

In fact, the problems are intimately connected. They are aspects of a single process: the violent shuddering to a halt of the long boom and the onset of the most severe crisis since the war.

The crisis is rooted in the over-accumulation of capital. While its diverse manifestations are not simply passive reflections of over-accumulation, their development and significance are primarily structured by it. The links can be thought of in terms of the metaphor Marx used to illustrate the relationship between the economy and other aspects of society. Thus accumulation is the base underlying the economic superstructure of international currency movements, stock-exchange deals and so on. The former is ultimately determinant but no one-to-one relationship exists between changes at different levels.

The high rate of accumulation underlying the boom absorbed large quantities of labour power. By the end of the 1950s, the industrial reserve army had been exhausted in the advanced capitalist countries with the exception of the USA. During the

Table 1

Unemployment as a percentage of the labour force(5)			
	1950	*1960*	*1970*
Germany	8.0	1.0	0.6
Italy	0.7 (1954)	3.9	3.1
France	1.6 (1954)	1.2	1.7
UK	1.3	1.3	2.2
USA	5.1	5.3	4.8

Artisans and peasants as a percentage of civilian employment(6)			
	1950	*1960*	*1970*
Germany	30.8	22.3	16.9
Japan	57.0 (1953)	46.6	35.0
Italy	45.3 (1954)	41.6	31.7
France	35.7 (1954)	30.5	22.2
UK	8.2	7.4	7.8
USA	20.3	16.1	10.2

Percentage of women aged 25-64 in the labour force (7)		
	1960	*1970*
Germany	43.7	45.9
France	42.0	47.0
UK	41.5	49.3
USA	40.4	48.0

Newly entering foreign workers (thousands)(8)			
	1958	*1965*	*1970*
UK	41.5	48.9	47.7
Germany	54.6	524.9	713.9
France	146.3	283.6	309.3

Total net immigration 1957-68 inclusive (thousands) (9)			
USA	4439	Germany	3014
France	2497	UK	140

1960s, accumulation depended on a flow of new workers from the shrinking peasant and artisanal sectors, increased employment of women and mass immigration. The latter became particularly important, assuming unprecedented proportions. (Table 1).

While these sources of additional labour power allowed high rates of accumulation to be maintained for some years, they did not fully alleviate the shortage of labour. Wages rose, eating into the rate of exploitation and reducing surplus value. Profitability declined (Table 2(a)).

This had a significant effect on accumulation in Europe and Japan. But this was offset to a considerable extent by a growth in United States investment associated with the Vietnam war. (Table 2(c)).

In the early 1970s, over-accumulation gave rise to a major slump. From mid-1974 to the time of writing (July 1977), about 15 million people have been without jobs in advanced capitalist countries and around 25 per cent of machinery has lain idle. The immediate causes of this stupendous waste of resources are a collapse of investment and consequent realisation difficulties. (Table 2(c)).

But why was this state of affairs allowed to develop, let alone persist? Why did governments not make good deficiencies in expenditure resulting from capitalists' failure to invest? Why were keynesian measures not used to prevent the slump?

Such policies were implemented in the early 1970s. A significant slowdown in economic growth began in mid-1969. From then until the middle of 1971, world capitalist output grew at less than one per cent a year. Governments in all major countries responded by initiating keynesian measures in the summer of 1971. The next 18 months saw an extremely dramatic boom. Output grew at a rate of nine per cent a year.

But the boom was short lived. When demand expanded, capitalists brought idle machinery back into operation and increased production rapidly in the short term. But they did not invest in new capacity (Table 2(c)). They preferred to buy office blocks or cocoa crops yet to be harvested in the hope of a quick killing when prices rose. Thus the 'mini-boom' brought an orgy of speculation but little expansion of the productive forces. It came to a sharp halt at the end of 1973. Keynesian policies were abandoned.

Expanding markets had proved an insufficient incentive. Capitalists were not prepared to accumulate because they did not expect to be able to produce additional commodities profitably. There was good reason for this pessimism. Profits had not recovered despite increased opportunities for sales. In a number of countries, they had declined still further (Table 2(b)).

Table 2

(a) Profits as a percentage of output(10)

	1951	1960	1970	1973	1974	1975
USA	25.9	19.6	15.2	17.7	14.1	15.6
Japan	31.8	39.2	34.4	26	17	–
UK	30.8	27.4	16.1	17.7	9.7	6.9
Italy	24.2	16.5	11.0	3.6	3.4	–
Germany	34.4	29.3	23.5	20	18	18

(b) Rates of profit(11)

USA	7.9	5.3	5.4	–	–
UK	8.3	3.7	3.9	3.5	3
France	8.3	7.9	7.1	5.0	1.4

(c) Average annual percentage rate of growth of investment(12)

	USA	Japan	France	Germany	Italy	UK	Europe
1951-59	2.5	11.8	–	–	–	–	7.0
1959-64	3.5	19.2	–	–	–	–	8.4
1964-69	4.6	14.2	–	–	–	–	4.8
1969-73	5.4	11.6	–	–	–	–	4.9
1973-76	0.7	−7.4	0	−1.8	−2.4	−4.8	–

This experience brings out clearly the limits of keynesianism. While it can alleviate difficulties in the *realisation* of surplus value, it can do nothing to ease problems in its *production*. In the present crisis, the fall in profitability resulting from over-accumulation is the fundamental factor underlying deficiencies in expenditure. To the extent that keynesian policies succeed in increasing production and employment, they actually intensify this underlying problem.

This analysis renders intelligible the prolonged slump of the last few years. The capitalist class would not necessarily benefit from the implementation of policies designed to expand the economy. A boom would certainly have some advantages. It would increase markets, allow idle machinery to be used again and thus increase total profits in the short run. But it would also have disadvantages. Most importantly, by raising employment, it would worsen the pressure on the rate of surplus value and thus work to prevent the rate of profit from rising in the medium and longer term.

Similarly, a prolongation or deepening of the slump would also have contradictory effects for capital. The resulting unemployment would work to hold down wages and thus help in achieving an increase in the rate of exploitation. But the restriction of markets would prevent any improvement in the conditions for realisation. Without a rise in wages, capitalists producing means of subsistence would not find it worthwhile to invest because they could not sell the extra output without reducing prices. Without the likelihood of increased sales to these capitalists, those producing means of production would equally have no incentive to expand capacity.

The capitalist class appears to face an insoluble contradiction. The re-creation of conditions for the profitable expansion of production requires an improvement in the prospects for both producing and realising surplus value. Any policy which works to improve one simultaneously acts to worsen the other. For the class as a whole, this is indeed so.

But the contradiction does not exist for an individual capitalist. Reductions in his workers' wages improve the conditions for producing surplus value without worsening those for realising it. This is because expenditure by his work force constitutes a negligible proportion of total spending. If he can reduce costs sufficiently, he can lower prices, gain an increased share of the market and make high profits at the expense of his rivals. Marx expressed this as follows: each capitalist would like his workers' wages to be as low as possible (to minimise costs) and those of his competitors to be as high as possible (to maximise markets).

On an international scale, the capitalist class of a single country is in this respect analogous to an individual capitalist. If its costs can be brought below those of foreign competitors, markets abroad can provide the basis for a profitable expansion of production.

Thus it is in the interests of each national capitalist class to exert pressure on its state to do everything possible to hold down wages. This includes the use of keynesian policies *in reverse* - the reduction of state expenditure to generate unemployment. By and large, this has been the position adopted in recent years by capitalists throughout Europe, North America and Japan.

In reality, of course, it is no more possible for every national capitalist class to solve its problems in this way than for every participant to win a boxing match. But that does not stop them trying. The results include a buffeting for the international trade and payments system, continued worldwide slump and the aiming of repeated body blows against the working class in each country.

3. Social Democracy in Crisis

The fortunes of social democracy tend to follow those of capitalism. When accumulation proceeds smoothly, social-democratic perspectives appear plausible and their proponents gain influence in workers' parties. In a crisis, on the other hand, social democracy finds its prognoses rendered obsolete by events and its policies unworkable. Disagreements arise in its ranks and working-class support falls off.

During the post-war boom, rapid development of the productive forces provided the basis for full employment, rising incomes and expanding social services. The boom appeared to confirm the belief that keynesianism could ensure crisis-free expansion and thus to vindicate social-democratic emphasis on the distribution of output. Capitalism's ability to deliver the goods and social democracy's apparent ability to both explain and adapt to this won the latter substantial working-class support.

Today, Crosland's fairy godmother has obviously failed. The slump brings the limits of keynesianism home to workers more effectively than could any marxist theoretician. It shows clearly that capitalism's inability to sustain effective utilisation and development of the productive forces is a more fundamental problem than is distributional inequality.

The share of output consumed by the British working class rose from 69.3 per cent in 1955 to 73.7 per cent in 1972. In historical terms, this was a substantial redistribution. Production grew by 51.8 per cent over the same period. Workers' living standards therefore rose by 62.8 per cent, of which 11 percentage points are attributable to a change in the distribution of output and 51.8 percentage points to an increase in the total.[13] During the boom, the effect of the development of the productive forces dwarfed that of redistribution.

In the slump, productive forces have lain idle. At the time of writing (July 1977) sufficient unused machinery and unemployed workers exist in Britain to increase output by approximately 20 per cent. Luxury consumption by the rich, on the other hand, absorbs at most five per cent of production. Thus, today, the full utilisation of existing productive forces could yield considerably greater increases in workers' living standards than could further redistribution.

Such an increase in output would permit 50 per cent more industrial investment (to develop future productive forces), a doubling of housebuilding, a 10 per cent rise in health and education provision, a 50 per cent increase in pensions and other benefits, a minimum wage of £70 per week for both sexes and a further five per cent increase in workers' living standards.[14] These are not alternatives. They could all be achieved simultaneously.

This list is one way of expressing the costs of unemployment. As such, it is a narrowly-economic, minimum estimate of the price paid by the working class today for the maintenance of an outmoded system.

As the slump exposes the theoretical bankruptcy of post-war social democracy, even support gained during the boom comes to present problems. Workers' parties now form all or a part of the government in a number of countries. This puts them on the spot. In opposition, such parties can claim that economic difficulties are either exaggerated or the result of incompetent government. They can continue to offer social-democratic programmes devised during the boom without the constraint of having to implement them. In office, they face a harsher reality.

The crisis thus compels reformist parties to switch ground. There are essentially only two possible ways to move. In recent years almost all such parties have toyed with both. Many have been severely weakened by internal divisions over which to choose.

One alternative is to adopt the capitalists' strategy. This involves abandoning any perspective of immediate improvements in living standards and, instead, opting for policies designed to reduce them. The rationale for such a move is essentially the same as that offered by the capitalist class: the possibility of reducing costs, raising profitability, increasing sales abroad and thereby re-establishing the conditions for sustained accumulation. This, it is argued, is the only way to lay the basis for future reforms. This approach can conveniently be termed *right reformism*.

Such 'reformism without reforms' is well illustrated by the policies of the Labour government from mid-1974 to the time of writing. These have included savage cuts in social service expenditure and incomes policies designed to reduce real wages. The justification used throughout has been the possibility of an 'export-led boom', supposedly always just around the corner.

These policies have brought unemployment for two million people and a fall in real wages for the average manual worker over the last two years of 16 per cent, or £10 a week.[15] This is a bigger wage cut than has occurred in any other two year period this century. It makes Crosland's 'threshold of mass abundance' seem a little remote.

Not surprisingly, the leadership of a party adopting such policies tends to lose working-class support. This is evidenced inside the Labour Party in abstentions or votes against the government by back benchers and in attempts at constituency level to oust right-reformist MPs. Dwindling support for Labour from the working class as a whole shows clearly in by-election results and in growing hostility to incomes policies among trade unionists.

The other option open to a reformist party is to press for policies which will work to defend workers' immediate interests. This implies opposition to cuts in social service expenditure, support for programmes aimed to reduce unemployment and so on. Those who believe such policies capable either of re-stabilising capitalism or of gradually introducing socialism can conveniently be termed *left reformists*.

A left reformist approach is contained in the Labour Party's *Programme 1973* and in its two 1974 election manifestos. As the Labour government has moved to the right, this position has been maintained by Tony Benn and his supporters and by the group around the *Tribune* newspaper.

As living standards continue to fall without any improvement in the economic situation materialising, support for left reformists grows. Since they offer a more radical programme than right reformists, they appeal particularly to politically advanced workers. It is therefore important to examine the perspective left reformism offers to the labour movement.

Since the assessment of left reformism presented below is largely a negative one, it is important to make clear that the criticisms are offered in a different spirit to that with which right reformism was approached. Regardless of the motivations of particular individuals, right reformism embodies directly anti-working class policies whereas left reformism represents an attempt to defend workers' interests, albeit an ultimately misguided one. While right reformism should be treated with outright hostility by socialists of all persuasions, left reformism should be approached in a spirit of fraternal if unrelenting criticism. To hold back on such criticism would be to demean a vital objective shared by marxists and many left reformists: the political development of the labour movement.

Some left reformists argue in keynesian terms. They point out that cuts in government spending and in real wages reduce overall expenditure, intensify the problem of markets and thus hinder recovery. This analysis is the opposite side of the coin to that of right reformists and capitalists.

Both sides emphasise one aspect of the difficulties capitalism faces. Right reformists concentrate on problems in the production of surplus value while these left reformists consider only those of realisation. But right reformism does at least hold out the hope of a solution to the problem of markets: the much vaunted expansion of exports. Keynesianism offers no solution to the problem of profitability.

But not all left reformists rely on keynesianism. The more sophisticated offer a more radical analysis and programme. This 'alternative economic strategy', which has widespread support in the labour movement, is most ably argued for by Stuart Holland in *Strategy for Socialism* and *The Socialist Challenge*.

Holland's approach differs considerably from those of his social-democratic predecessors. In part, this results from his more thorough grasp of antagonistic class interests. But it is also partly a result of different economic circumstances. Bernstein and Crosland wrote during periods of capitalist stability. The priorities for them were to criticise marxist approaches emphasising the inevitability of crises and to evolve a political strategy relevant to what they saw as a new, crisis-free epoch. Writing during a crisis, Holland faces different tasks. He is consequently more critical of Crosland than of Marx.

Holland is contemptuous of Crosland's emphasis of redistribution. He argues that distributional inequalities 'stem essentially from the structure of power and unequal incomes necessary for the functioning of a capitalist system'. He is equally scathing about keynesianism. His critique of this takes us to the core of his analysis.

Both Bernstein and Crosland argued that a new development in capitalism ensured a crisis-free future. Holland turns this, the normal pattern of social-democratic analysis, on its head. He argues that recent instability is the product of a new stage of capitalism. At first glance this seems to place him closer to Lenin than to Bernstein or Crosland.

The superficial similarity extends further. Like Lenin in his day, Holland locates the cause of instability in the concentration and centralisation of capital. This has reached the point, he argues, where industries are dominated by a few giant firms whose operations span many countries. These *multi-national companies* are sufficiently powerful to evade both the normal pressure of the law of value and attempts by the state to regulate the economy along keynesian lines.

Where production is carried out by numerous small firms, each has a negligible influence on overall output. If 1000 firms each produce 10 pairs of shoes a week, for example, the effect on total supply of one doubling its output is minimal. Price depends on the overall balance between supply and demand and, as firms are free to move between industries, tends to settle at the level yielding the average rate of profit (see chapter 3).

If, on the other hand, five firms each produce 2000 pairs of shoes, one can influence total supply and hence price. If a single firm doubles its output, supply increases by 20 per cent and price falls. Profits decline unless and until some capital leaves the industry.

Multi-nationals are aware, Holland argues, of the dangers of excessive production and of competition among themselves for market shares. They therefore operate to avoid them. They do not raise production rapidly. They hesitate to introduce technical innovations which would increase output. If one raises prices, others follow. If new capital moves into the industry, prices are reduced until the new entrant is driven out. So even without the explicit collusion of cartels, the normal operation of the law of value and consequent pressure to accumulate are frustrated. The productive forces stagnate.

It is the size and international scope of these firms' operations which, in Holland's view, prevents the state from effectively influencing their behaviour by keynesian methods. For example, an expansion of domestic markets need not lead to an expansion of production within the country. Multi-nationals produce where it is cheapest to do so. Since keynesian increases in expenditure will not improve the relative costs of producing in a country, they are as likely to increase exports to it as investment within it.

This analysis provides the justification for a considerably more radical programme than those put forward by either social democrats during the boom or right reformists today. The most important proposals are those for large-scale nationalisations, compulsory planning agreements and import controls.

The state is to take over at least one leading company in each industry. Once nationalised, these firms are to implement policies designed to re-establish effective competition. Prices will not simply be kept in line with those charged by other firms. Innovative investment will be undertaken, forcing competitors to follow suit. In short, state companies will act to re-introduce the normal operation of the law of value and compulsion to accumulate.

The threat of further nationalisations will persuade other large firms to participate in planning agreements: plans for production, investment, pricing and so on to be negotiated with the government. Planning agreements are intended to help re-establish the pressure to accumulate and to reduce disruptions arising from the anarchy of capitalist production. They represent a half-way house between central planning and unfettered market forces. Most firms remain in private hands but are compelled to comply with government policy.

Imports are to be selectively restricted on the basis of information about trade between home and foreign branches of firms obtained during planning-agreement negotiations. These controls are intended to prevent government policy being either sabotaged by the use firms make of foreign branches or unnecessarily hampered by 'genuine' foreign competition. Thus, paradoxically, while domestic competition is to be increased to facilitate the functioning of the law of value nationally, the economy is to be insulated from the international operation of the law.

Left reformists offer this programme as a solution to workers' problems. They claim that it can protect the working class in the crisis while simultaneously opening a path to socialism. This claim is false.

Seeing these policies as a step towards socialism involves a mis-estimation of the role parliamentary democracy can play in social revolution. Holland casts it in the leading part. He foresees an extension of nationalisation and a tightening of planning agreements gradually wresting power from the capitalist class.

In reality, capitalists would never submit to slow euthanasia. They would stop producing, ship assets abroad and do everything in their power to sabotage government policy. Economic and social chaos would result, opening the way to political reaction and all-out assaults on the working class. The 1973 Chilean coup - mounted against an elected government attempting to carry out a programme similar to Holland's - provides a bloody object-lesson in this regard.

This aspect of left reformism holds great dangers for the labour movement. By suggesting that socialism can be achieved in this way, it encourages workers to subordinate the industrial struggle to the parliamentary one. In a crisis, any weakening of trade unions - the most powerful of working-class organisations - invites moves towards totalitarianism.

The left reformists' other fundamental error is a misunderstanding of the crisis. A correct appreciation of this shows their programme to be incapable of protecting jobs and living standards.

Holland's analysis of the crisis is seriously deficient. The argument that multi-nationals do not invest in Britain because costs - crucially wages and tax rates - are lower elsewhere squares awkwardly with the facts. British wage levels are among the lowest in Europe and taxation on capital is negative (subsidies exceed taxes). More fundamentally, choices about *where* to invest can hardly explain a *worldwide* collapse.

The crucial factor missing from Holland's account is profitability. In his lengthier book he acknowledges a decline in profits but minimises its scale and significance. He does not mention it in the shorter version. In fact, the whole tenor of the argument is that multi-nationals make enormous profits. In emphasising deviations from the normal functioning of the law of value, he sweeps under the carpet the more fundamental problem generated by its operation - over-accumulation.

Holland's analysis thus shares essential features with keynesianism. Both locate the cause of the slump in capitalists' failure to invest. Neither acknowledges the decline in profitability lying behind this.

By ignoring profitability, Holland is able to claim, in company with keynesians, that capitalist stability can be restored without attacking jobs, living standards or working conditions. For him, the fundamental problem is the rise of multi-nationals which has thwarted the normal operation of the law of value and compulsion to accumulate. If his policies were implemented, these pressures would be re-established. Decisive state action could therefore end the slump and ensure crisis-free development in future. The fairy godmother is re-habilitated. Only the magical wand has changed - planning agreements replace public works.

These crucial weaknesses - seeing parliamentary democracy as the vehicle for introducing socialism and believing capitalism capable, with or without a little help from the state, of indefinite development of the productive forces - did not originate with left reformism. They are central threads linking Bernstein's, Crosland's and Holland's ideas and dividing them off from marxism. Despite radical rhetoric and hostility to its theoretical predecessors, left reformism has failed to break out of the strait-jacket of social-democratic tradition. This is, in the last analysis, why it has been unable to offer a viable strategy to the working class.

The crisis has given reformism quite a buffeting. It has exposed the theoretical bankruptcy of Crosland and his followers and posed their successors problems which they are incapable of solving. The movement is divided on analysis and policy. Organisational splits may follow. Neither wing offers a programme adequate to workers' needs.

This opens up enormous possibilities. The slump has confirmed marxist prognoses of crisis. Reformism's inability to offer a realistic way forward has weakened its political hold on the working class. The opportunity exists, for perhaps the first time for a generation, of winning large sections of the labour movement to a revolutionary socialist perspective.

Notes and References

For full details of titles see Bibliography, page 163.

1. Politics, Economics and History

1. Marx seldom if ever referred to himself as a socialist. He preferred to call himself a communist to distinguish his ideas from those of the bourgeois socialists. Similarly, he called the social system that we would today refer to as socialism the first or lower phase of communism. Engels sometimes referred to marxism as scientific socialism.
2. *The Communist Manifesto*, p.106.
3. *ibid*. p.116-17.
4. *ibid*. p.106-07.
5. *ibid*. p.117.
6. *ibid*. p.113-14.
7. There was something of a revival of utopianism in the late 1960s — people going off to Wales to grow their own stereo systems and so on. Needless to say, it was short-lived.
8. The theory's title can, alternatively, be analysed to reveal its polemical significance. Looked at in this way, *materialism* is aimed at Hegel, from whose theory of history Marx derived a good deal, but who had ultimately to be rejected because he did not begin from the real interaction between human beings and nature. *Historical* is directed against Ricardo, whose economic writings were also influential in the development of Marx's ideas, but whose central weakness — like that of the proudhonists, who adopted some of his ideas in a vulgarised form — was the failure to see capitalism as a limited stage in historical development.

2. Simple Commodity Production

1. There are cases of transformed nature which are not use values because no one wants them. The most important examples are waste by-products generated in the production of other goods.
2. Commodity production is anarchic in the sense that it is not consciously planned. This does not imply that it is not subject to regulating laws. One task of marxist economics is the discovery of such laws.
3. It may be argued that some people are intrinsically more suited to some jobs than to others - nimble fingered people to being tailors and those with a large build to being blacksmiths. In so far as this is true, there need be no problem as long as a reasonable proportion of the population is endowed with each skill. In any case the point is greatly exaggerated: nimbleness of fingers and strength of muscles are largely *acquired* in the course of doing jobs which require them.
4. This unrealistic but numerically simple example serves to illustrate the basic principle. Complications arise from the fact that teaching labour will be equivalent to more than one hour of unskilled labour and from the use in training of commodities such as tools which are themselves the product of human labour, some of which may be skilled. Thus tools and teaching labour have themselves to be 'reduced' to units of unskilled labour time.

3. Exploitation and Surplus Value

1. For an attempt at an analysis of the social relations under which the reproduction of labour power takes place see Harrison.
2. *Capital*, vol. 1, p.280.
3. The sex of individual workers and capitalists is irrelevant in this context. Unfortunately the English language requires that one be specified. Since it might be confusing to switch between sexes - suggesting that whether a particular

individual in an example is male or female is significant -
and writing 'she or he' and 'his or her' all the time makes for
clumsy sentences I have stuck to the male sex throughout
the rest of the book.
4. *Value Studies*, p.205.

4. Living with Commodities

1. *Surveys from Exile*, p.144.
2. The *extent* of exploitation may be less obvious. If serfs take
   corn they grow on their own land to the lord's mill for grind-
   ing and he keeps some grain in 'payment', some labour
   performed on the serfs' own land is producing a surplus for
   the lord.
3. In practice, agreements involving trade unions do have a
   somewhat different legal status in some capitalist countries.
   This is a result of class struggle (see below) and is at odds
   with the fundamental principles of bourgeois legality.

6. Rotten Capitalism

1. *The Communist Manifesto*, p.86.
2. For a survey of the breakdown controversy see Sweezy.
3. The two approaches are not inconsistent. Rosa Luxemburg
   adopted both: arguing that breakdown was inevitable
   (especially in *The Accumulation of Capital*) and that
   capitalism had entered the phase in which it was no longer
   historically progressive (especially in *Reform or Revolution*, written in reply to Bernstein). But an adequate demonstration of either would have been a sufficient answer to
   Bernstein.
4. Quoted in Sweezy, p.252.

7. Capitalism since the War

1. Figures for the capitalist world are for the *Organisation for*

Economic Co-operation and Development (OECD) as a whole. This comprises twenty-four countries, including all major capitalist powers.

2. The term gives too much credit to Keynes: many of the ideas are foreshadowed in Marx's writings and were developed independently of Keynes and in a theoretically superior form by Michael Kalecki.

3. Crosland was unable to devise a satisfactory name for this mythical, new, non-capitalist society. He could not call it socialism because, like Bernstein, he did not conceive of socialism as a type of society but only as the policies and ideals of a movement.

4. Crosland's book was concerned exclusively with Britain, where universal adult suffrage had existed since 1929. But it was a more recent and incomplete victory for social democracy as a whole, being first introduced in France, Italy and Japan in the immediate post-war period.

5. Obtained from relevant OECD *Labour Force Statistics*.

6. Self-employment as a percentage of civilian-employment. Source as note five.

7. *Towards full employment and price stability*, OECD 1977.

8. *Bohning*, tables 3.2, 3.3, 3.4 and 3.8.

9. *ibid*.

10. Manufacturing profits as a percentage of manufacturing output. Obtained from relevant *National Accounts* of each country. The figures are not strictly comparable across countries because of differences in definition.

11. After-tax profits for industrial and commercial companies expressed as a percentage of capital employed. Figures obtained from *Brookings Papers 1974, No. 1* (USA) *I.N.S.E.E.* (France) and *Bank of England Quarterly Bulletin*, March 1976 (UK). Again figures are not strictly comparable across countries.

12. Private investment excluding housebuilding. Obtained from relevant OECD *National Accounts* and *Economic Outlooks*.

13. The share of output consumed by the working class is

defined as after-tax wages and salaries plus that part of government expenditure consumed by workers. The figures are taken from Glyn (1975) which explains the assumptions and method of calculation more fully. The growth in output is taken from UK *National Accounts*.

14. This calculation is taken from Glyn (1977) which explains the assumptions and method of calculation.

15. Source: *Incomes Data Services*. The figure of £10 is at current prices.

Guide to Further Reading

For full details of titles see Bibliography, page 163.

The best book on marxist economics is *Capital*. It *is* difficult, but no more so than many of the recent textbook introductions. It is also far more interesting than most of them. It is best read in a study group.

Otherwise, the best single book is *Sweezy*. It is lively, aware of the political relevance of the subject and clear. It has not been surpassed in the thirty-five years since it was written.

There has been a revival of debate on marxist economics in recent years. In Britain, much of it has taken place in the *Bulletin of the Conference of Socialist Economists*, recently re-named *Capital and Class*.

Chapter 1: The discussion of the socialists is largely based on the *Communist Manifesto*, the most important single text for chapters one and five. The best political biography of Marx in English is *Nicolaievsky and Maenchen-Helfen*. Marx's best known statement on historical materialism is in the preface to *A Contribution to the Critique of Political Economy*. *Mehring* is useful. A stimulating if somewhat abstruse discussion of some of the central concepts can be found in *Balibar*.

Chapter 2: Most of the analysis here is based on the first hundred pages or so of volume one of *Capital*. A thorough, if quite difficult, discussion of this - in many ways the most difficult part of *Capital* - is contained in *Rubin*. The concept of value and the workings of the law of value are introduced clearly

In the early chapters of *Sweezy*. The Robinson Crusoe parable is shamelessly plagiarised from *Kay*. *Nicolaus* is good on the relationship between bourgeois socialism and artisanal production.

Chapter 3: The core of the analysis comes from parts two and three of volume one of *Capital*. Again, *Sweezy's* exposition is clear. Anyone intrigued by or sceptical about the relationship between prices of production and values should consult chapter seven of *Sweezy*. The opening paragraphs of section three draw heavily on *Rowthorn*.

Chapter 4: Marx's basic ideas on fetishism are contained in a brilliant short section in volume one of *Capital* (chapter one section four). The exposition here largely follows *Geras* (1972). For a currently fashionable critique of the theory see *Brewster*. On section three see *Capital*, volume one, section six; on section two watch television for an evening.

Chapter 5: On capitalism's progressive role see *The Communist Manifesto*. On changes in the labour process see chapters 13, 14 and 15 of volume one of *Capital*. On Marx's politics of the period see *Nicolaievsky and Maenchen-Helfen*.

Chapter 6: *Sweezy* contains a full and informed discussion of accumulation and crises but the defence of underconsumptionalism relies on quite arbitrary assumptions. For a vigorous if logically deficient defence of the 'increase in constant capital per worker' thesis see *Yaffe*. A formal proof of the effect of new techniques on the rate of profit can be found in *Glyn* (1973). For a position close to the one argued here see *Itoh*. Section two is largely based on *Bernstein, Bukharin* and *Lenin*. *Colletti* contains an interesting discussion; for section three see *Bernstein, Lenin, Luxemburg* (1970) and *Trotsky*. *Geras* (1975) does an excellent job of disentangling the shifting positions held by leading marxists around this time.

Chapter 7: *Crosland* is well worth wading through. *Sutcliffe* is a witty exposition and critique of keynesianism. For a selection of marxist attempts to explain the boom see *Baran and Sweezy, Kidron* and *Mandel*. Sadly, there is, as yet, little worth reading on the crisis. Holland's shorter book - *Strategy for Socialism* - is sufficient to get an idea of his views. *Glyn* (1977) provides a good critique.

It is tempting to end with a list of books to avoid. But space is limited.

Bibliography

Balibar, E. 'The basic concepts of historical materialism', in
Althusser, L. and Balibar, E. *Reading Capital*, London:
New Left Books 1970.

Baran, P. and Sweezy, P. *Monopoly Capital*, New York:
Monthly Review Press 1964.

Bernstein, E. *Evolutionary Socialism*, New York: Schocken
1961.

Bohning, W. *The Migration of Workers in the UK and the
European Community*, Oxford: OUP 1972.

Brewster, B. 'Fetishism in *Capital* and *Reading Capital*',
Economy and Society, August 1976.

Bukharin, N. *Imperialism and World Economy*, London:
Merlin Press 1972.

Bulletin of the Conference of Socialist Economists, London:
CSE four-monthly, 1971-76.

Capital and Class, London: CSE four-monthly, 1977-

Colletti, L. 'Bernstein and the marxism of the Second International', in Colletti, L. *From Rousseau to Lenin*,
London: New Left Books 1972.

Crosland, A. *The Future of Socialism*, London: Jonathan
Cape 1956.

Geras, N. (1972) 'Marx and the critique of political economy'
in Blackburn, R. (ed.) in *Ideology in Social Science*, London:
Fontana 1972.
(1975) 'Between the Russian revolutions' in *New Left Review*,
January/February 1975. Reprinted in Geras, N. *The Legacy
of Rosa Luxemburg*, London: New Left Books 1975.

Glyn, A. (1973) 'Productivity, organic composition and the falling rate of profit - a reply', *Bulletin of the Conference of Socialist Economists*, Autumn 1973.
(1975) 'Notes on the profits squeeze', *Bulletin of the Conference of Socialist Economists,* February 1975.
(1977) *Capitalist Crisis; 'Alternative Strategy': Socialist Plan*, (provisional title), London: Militant 1978.

Harrison, J. 'The political economy of housework', *Bulletin of the Conference of Socialist Economists*, Winter 1973.

Holland, S. *The Socialist Challenge*, London: Quartet 1977.
Strategy for Socialism, London: Spokesman Books 1975.

Itoh, M. 'The Formation of Marx's theory of crisis', *Bulletin of the Conference of Socialist Economists*, February 1975.

Kay, G. *Development and Underdevelopment. A Marxist Analysis*, London: Macmillan 1975.

Kidron, M. *Western Capitalism Since the War*, London: Weidenfeld and Nicolson 1968.

Lenin, V. *Imperialism, the Highest Stage of Capitalism*, Peking: Foreign Languages Press 1965.

Luxemburg, R. (1963) *The Accumulation of Capital*, London: Routledge and Kegan Paul 1963.
(1970) *Reform or Revolution*, New York: Pathfinder Press 1970.

Mandel, E. *Late Capitalism*, London: New Left Books 1975.

Mehring, F. *On Historical Materialism*, London: New Park Publications 1975.

Marx, K. *Capital*, I, London: Penguin 1976.
A Contribution to the Critique of Political Economy, London: Lawrence and Wishart 1971.
Surveys from Exile, London: Penguin 1973.
Value Studies, London: New Park Publications 1976.

Marx, K. and Engels F. *The Communist Manifesto*, London: Penguin 1967.

Nicolaus, M. 'Forward', in Marx, K. (Nicolaus, N. ed.), *Grundrisse*, London: Penguin 1973.

Nicolaievsky, B. and Maenchen-Helfen, O. *Karl Marx: Man and Fighter*, London: Penguin 1970.

Rowthorn, B. 'Vulgar Economy (part two)', *Bulletin of the Conference of Socialist Economists*, Spring 1973.

Rubin, I. *Essays on Marx's Theory of Value*, Detroit: Black and Red 1972.

Sweezy, P. *The Theory of Capitalist Development*, London: Monthly Review Press 1968.

Sutcliffe, B. 'Keynesianism and the stabilisation of capitalist economies' in Green, F. and Nore, P. (eds.), *Economics: An Anti-Text*, London: Macmillan 1977.

Trotsky, L. *The Permanent Revolution and Results and Prospects*, London: New Park Publications 1962.

Yaffe, D. 'The marxian theory of crisis, capital and the state', *Bulletin of the Conference of Socialist Economists*, Winter 1972.

Index

This index contains entries for proper names, subjects discussed and concepts employed. In the case of the latter, only pages in which the concept is introduced or further developed are cited. There are no entries for capitalism, Marx, marxism or Proudhon.